# ESSAYS
## that will get you into
# College

*Adrienne Dowhan, Chris Dowhan, and Dan Kaufman*

## BARRON'S

*All inquiries should be addressed to:*
Barron's Educational Series, Inc.
250 Wireless Boulevard
Hauppauge, New York 11788
**www.barronseduc.com**

*Library of Congress Control Number: 2009013487*

ISBN-13: 978-0-7641-4210-9
ISBN-10: 0-7641-7-4210-0

**Library of Congress Cataloging-in-Publication Data**

Kaufman, Daniel, 1968-
    Essays that will get you into college / Dan Kaufman, Chris Dowhan
and Adrienne Dowhan.—3rd ed.
        p.   cm.
    Includes index.
    ISBN-13: 978-0-7641-4210-9
    ISBN-10: 0-7641-4210-0
    1. College applications—United States.   2. Exposition (Rhetoric)
    3. Academic writing.   I. Dowhan, Chris.   II. Dowhan, Adrienne.
    III. Title.
    LB2351.52.U6K38 2009
    808'.066378—dc22
                                                    2009013487

Printed in the United States of America
9 8 7 6 5 4 3 2 1

# Contents

## PART ONE
# Preparation   1

## PART TWO
# Strategy   33

# Acknowledgments

The authors of this book are all part of an Internet-based company called IvyEssays. Since its creation in 1996, IvyEssays' goal has been to help students gain admission to leading colleges and graduate schools by providing them with a variety of resources. These include examples of previously successful essays and professional editing services. We are extremely happy to be working with Barron's on this book series, which will put our extensive information and advice into print for university applicants.

We owe our sincere thanks to two groups of people. First, we thank all of the students who have permitted us to publish their admissions essays so that they might help illuminate the way for future rounds of hopeful applicants. Second, we thank the team of IvyEssays contributors, made up of past and present admissions officers and professional writers who together have logged over 50 years of admissions experience. This series would not have been possible without the assistance of those listed below:

**Thomas Vance Sturgeon** has over eight years of experience in the admissions process as Associate Director of Admission at Duke University and Assistant Director of Admission at Guilford College. Mr. Sturgeon is currently the Director of Admissions and College Placement at the South Carolina School for Science and Mathematics. Today, Mr. Sturgeon is a widely published author and lecturer on the subject of college admissions. He has been quoted in *Money Magazine's Guide to Colleges* and published in the *Journal of College Admissions*.

**Marcy Whaley** is the former Associate Director of Admissions at the California Institute of Technology and Assistant Dean of Admission at the Illinois Institute of Technology. She has over a decade of experience in college admissions and is currently an independent admissions consultant and freelance technical writer.

**Scott Anderson** is currently Associate Director of Admissions at Cornell University. Mr. Anderson's past experience includes the position of Assistant Director of Admission at Vassar College. He has also been on the admissions staffs at the University of Vermont, St. Michael's College, and the University of Virginia.

**Patricia M. Soares** is an independent educational consultant for underprivileged youth with years of experience as an admissions officer. She has been the Assistant Director of Admissions at Connecticut College and an admissions officer at Rhode Island College.

**Joanna Henderson** was the Director of Graduate Admissions responsible for MBA programs at Babson for four years and the Dean of Admissions at Colby-Sawyer College for five. She is currently the Director of the New England Admissions Office at Marietta College in Ohio and is an advisor/consultant for Stanley Kaplan Educational Center. She is the author of *ZINGERS! Creating Achievements from Ordinary Experiences,* published in 1988.

**Mirium Ruth Albert** is currently an Assistant Professor of Legal and Ethical Studies at Fordham University Schools of Business. She was a Legal Methods Professor and Associate Director of Admissions at Widener University School of Law. While there, she counseled prospective applicants and evaluated over 4,000 applications. She also taught an L.S.A.T. course for Stanley Kaplan Educational Center.

**Amy Engle** worked at the Hofstra University School of Law for more than seven years and served there as the Assistant Dean for Admissions.

**Helen LaFave** is currently an independent consultant who counsels prospective students through all stages of the admissions process. She has also served as Senior Programs Officer and Recruitment Program Officer at Columbia University. While there, she helped numerous students through extensive graduate school application processes.

**Ellen M. Watts** has worked in graduate admissions for nine years and is currently the Director of Admissions and Student Affairs at Columbia University School of Dental and Oral Surgery, where she screens over 2,000 applications annually. In addition, she serves as an independent admissions counselor, specializing in interview skills workshops.

**Amy Yerkes** was an Instructor at the University of Maryland School of Medicine where she taught a course designed to increase the writing skills of prospective medical students for the Office of Minority Student Affairs. She has also taught at the University of Pennsylvania and is currently Assistant to the Dean at Johns Hopkins University School of Continuing Studies and a Lecturer at Western Maryland College.

**IvyEssays** was founded based on the belief that some people have far more access than others to the resources and information that improve one's odds of getting into the top schools. While admissions officers do their best to take these disparities into account, students must equip themselves for the application process to the best of their abilities. IvyEssays hopes that its services can help level the admissions playing field by providing resources that might otherwise be available to only the more privileged. Good luck and good writing!

# Introduction

## The Competition

Unfortunately for today's applicants, getting into college has grown more competitive than ever. As the sons and daughters of the baby boomers graduate from high school and set their sights on a higher education, the nation's colleges and universities are becoming flooded with applications. Most admissions committees are seeing their highest number of applications ever. Schools that were not considered very selective a couple of years ago are now turning away highly qualified applicants because they simply do not have the space to accommodate them. Grades and S.A.T. scores are important. However, with so many qualified applicants now vying for a limited number of spots, they need a way to set themselves apart from the masses. The good news is that they DO have a way to sell themselves to the admissions committee. That opportunity lies in the essay.

## The Essays—Why All the Fuss?

How would you feel if getting into the school of your choice had nothing to do with your grades and your test scores? What if your accomplishments and class rank were irrelevant to the admissions process? Imagine for a moment that the only thing an admissions committee would ever see is your essay. The committee would have to make a decision that will change the rest of your life based on only one or two double-spaced pages.

Does this make you elated or nervous? A little of both? In any case, this should be your frame of mind during the writing process. Everything you have done up to now is completed—past tense. You could not change things if you wanted to, so stop worrying. However, even if you have strong test scores and a solid G.P.A., this is not the time to rest on your laurels. The essays lie ahead. Until you have completed them, you should treat the essays like they are the only thing that matters. As one admissions officer stated:

> *Students do have a lot of control. They feel it is all in our hands, but what they show us is up to them. They shouldn't underestimate the importance of this.*

## Are the Essays Really That Important?

The answer is yes! However, do not take our word for it. Listen to an admissions officer:

*While at Duke, I did a study of how well single variables predicted an applicant's chances of admission. Being number one in the class gave an applicant about a 50–50 chance of getting in. Having a combined S.A.T. greater than 1,400 gave the student about a 65 percent chance. Receiving the highest score an admission officer could confer on an essay raised the odds to over 90 percent.*

Think of your essay as the face of your application. An application without an essay is a statistic—just another faceless person in a crowd. One committee member said:

*The application is a lifeless thing—a few sheets of paper and a few numbers. The essay is the best way to breathe life into it.*

An application with a poorly written essay does not give admissions officers the chance to care about you. Use simple psychology: Make them feel that they know you, and it will be harder for them to reject you. Make them know you *and like you,* and they might accept you despite your weakness in other areas.

Understanding the importance of the essays is a necessary first step toward perfecting your college application. However, that knowledge alone will not do you much good. In fact, it could even hurt your efforts if it only makes you nervous. So if all of this has you sweating, you can relax now. Taking the process seriously is the first step. We are here to help you get through the rest of them.

## How Will This Book Help?

We have developed a powerful program to help you write the most effective essays possible. We give you the tools that you need and couple them with a strategy that works. We will help you understand the goals of your essays, get the words onto paper, and polish them to perfection. Here is a taste of what you will find ahead:

1. **Preparation:** Before you can start writing, you need to understand your audience. (Who are those admissions officers, and what do they want?) You must also understand yourself to gather the material you will use to create colorful essays.

2. **Strategy:** Once you understand what is expected and are armed with plenty of potential material, you will need to develop a strategy. By using examples of essays that have worked in the past, we will help you decide how to focus your essays and how best to present them in light of the questions asked.

3. **The Essay:** When you have chosen a topic and know exactly what you want to say in your essay, you should begin typing. We will help you develop a structure, build powerful paragraphs and sentences, and create attention-grabbing opening lines. When you have presented your ideas in a solid first

draft, we will show you how to work it like a piece of clay, writing and rewriting until your essay is worthy of being the face of your application.

4. **A Graded Essay Section:** Before you can write "accept"able essays, you need to understand exactly what acceptable means to an admissions officer. In this section, we do not tell you what schools want to receive, we show you. This part presents 25 real essays graded and ranked by a panel of admissions officers from top schools across the country. We have included all their comments about what made the top ten essays so good and what could have been done to make the average ones even better.

5. **Interview Tips and Advice:** Because the interview holds so much in common with the essays, and because we had a panel of admissions officers ready and willing to give us tips and advice, we decided to turn the tables on our admissions team and interview the interviewers. The information presented here is based on what we learned about making the potentially nerve-shattering experience of interviewing a little easier.

Armed with this step-by-step program, you are sure to produce essays worthy of notice. Remember that your essays are the most important parts of your application right now because you can still control them. With that in mind, it is time to get started.

---

## A Note About Plagiarism

**Throughout this book, we have emphasized the need for honest, personal application essays. To submit anything else to an admissions team is not only stupid—it's illegal.**

If you do borrow material from other sources, be sure to credit it properly. If you are not careful about this, you may hurt your chances of getting into a particular school. To purposely avoid giving credit where credit is due is to court disaster.

In Chapter 1, an admissions officer is quoted as saying, "After fifteen years of reading hundreds of essays a year, you develop an amazing ability to see straight through the bull." This is also true of detecting plagiarism. Admissions officers do read hundreds of essays every year. In doing so, they have developed a sense of whether or not the author of the essay is being honest. Although it may sound impossible, these admissions officers also tend to remember many of the essays that they read. If it is discovered that you have "borrowed" someone else's essay, you will undoubtedly be denied admission.

You owe it to yourself to be honest, forthright, and sincere.

## PART ONE

# Preparation

Listen to how a top admissions officer described his view of the typical college applicant:

> *The deadline gets closer and the applicant is still sitting in that chair doing nothing and she's thinking to herself, "When I get it right in my head, then I'll write it down." She is guilty of two things. First, she hates the thought of writing about herself and she thinks that is a sufficient excuse not to write. But it's not. Second, she is hoping her dread will be subdued by inspiration, divine or otherwise, because she thinks that's what writers do. So she waits anxiously to be inspired. The worst writing ever set down was under the influence of inspiration.*

Does this sound familiar? If it does, what can you do about it? The same admissions officer continues:

> *Success is built on the completion of small, incremental steps. Ask any successful writer and they will tell you, "This is hard work."*

Get ready to embark on our own writing program of small, incremental steps designed to help you write the best essay possible. You will notice that by following this program, you will not actually start writing until more than halfway through the process. There is a reason for this. Good writing does not happen in a vacuum; it flows from solid research and preparation. The quality of any piece of writing relates directly to the thought that is put into it beforehand. An off-the-cuff response to an application question may contain good information and excellent snippets of writing, but it will almost certainly lack organization. You must organize your thoughts first and sift the good from bad, important from meaningless and interesting from banal.

This section leads you through the first two preparatory steps you will need to take. The first chapter, "Assess Your Audience," takes you inside the heads of the people who will be reading and judging your essays later—the admissions officers. Chapter 2, "Gather Your Material," shifts the focus to you. It offers brainstorming exercises intended to uncover the most colorful, distinctive facets of your character. It will give your thoughts—and your pen—the jump start they need to get things moving.

## CHAPTER 1

# Assess Your Audience

## Chapter Highlights

Committee members want to see the real you.

Essays can transform you from a statistic to a person.

Essays should be personal.

If your essays are not interesting, you will not make it past the first filter.

Essays that incorporate stories are well received—always tie the story to your theme.

Activities are more important in the essays than academic achievements and awards.

A personal essay does not have to be heavy or emotional.

Any subject that is meaningful to you can be made personal.

Choose topics that demonstrate how you are unique and how you may contribute.

If you address a weakness, attempt to demonstrate how you have improved.

Technical institutions (as well as their liberal arts counterparts) expect strong essays and look for well-rounded applicants.

*Dos and Don'ts Straight From the Admissions Committees:*

| | |
|---|---|
| Be yourself. | Don't be formal or predictable. |
| Be creative. | Don't expect a personal subject to make up for impersonal style. |
| Use humor. | Don't be dull. |
| Be honest. | Don't use words that you wouldn't use in normal conversation. |
| Use details. | Don't be vague or general. |
| Provide examples. | Don't make lists. |
| Get feedback. | Don't submit poorly constructed essays with errors. |

When we write, we imagine an audience, and consciously or not, we write for that audience. If you picture the admissions committee as a group of dry, nitpicky academics or solemn, medieval executioners, your essays will become dry, nitpicky, or solemn themselves. If you make this mistake, you will slowly but surely drain the humor, wit, and creativity straight out of your essays—the very ingredients essential for your success.

In this chapter, we take some time to get familiar with the real individuals who will be reading and evaluating your essays: who they are, what they look for in essays, and what they are tired of finding. Without having a clear understanding of your audience and their expectations, you risk writing to the stereotyped version of the committee created in your mind by anxiety and nervousness—which inevitably results in essays that lack color and focus.

## Profile of an Admissions Committee

One admissions committee member explained:

*The vast majority of admissions officers are "people persons." We shrink from using statistics in the admissions process and see those who rely on them as cold, calculating, and unconcerned with individuals. We are warm, friendly, helpful, eager to please, and anxious to keep a human face on this cumbersome process.*

Contrary to popular belief, admissions officers are not reading each file with a red pen in hand eager to place the next candidate into the rejection pile because of a few grammatical errors or a poorly chosen topic. Rather, they look forward to reading interesting, colorful essays written by real individuals. They want to like what they find when they open an application. One admissions officer said:

*Admissions people are student centered first. What we are trying to do is help students find the right match, the place where they will be the happiest. If our college isn't right for you, sometimes we will suggest another school or pass the name along. There is more cooperation than competition among the most prestigious schools. We do not have a gatekeeper mentality. We are not intent on rejecting applicants.*

The first people to read your application are the admissions assistants. It might surprise you to learn that this group is typically made up of recent college graduates—people only four or five years older than you. So if you want to know what they are *really* like, just look at your friends and their different personalities, interests and preferences, and then jump ahead five years.

If the assistants like your essay, they will pass it on to the associate directors. This middle tier of the committee reads only what the assistants pass along. Then the associate directors choose which essays to pass along to the director, who makes the final decision. So essentially, the mysterious group that holds your future in its hands is composed of a few recent grads of the college, a couple of associate directors, and a director who must evaluate thousands of applications in a month or two. They are bleary-eyed and overworked. Two of them explained:

*I can read three to four per hour depending upon the length and depth of each essay.*

*When pushed, I have read 30 in a day. That means that by the end of the day, I've developed a very low tolerance to nonsense.*

They read so many essays that sound like so many others that if your essay is original, if it contains thoughts, ideas, and experiences that are uniquely your own, it will make a vivid impression. They will thank you for it.

## How Important Are the Essays, Anyway?

One way to get inside the heads of admissions committees is to understand what is important to them. We asked our admissions panel to tell us what was the most important part of a student's application. They answered, "The essays." We asked them what aspects of the application students should focus on during their senior year. They answered, "The essays." We asked them over what part of the application process the students have the most control. The resounding reply was (big surprise), "The essays!"

You might think that if you are an exceptionally brilliant valedictorian with stellar scores and an abundance of honors and awards under your belt, the essays will play a lesser role in the overall admissions package. That is simply not true. While being top in your class is clearly going to give you an advantage, the fact is that over 20,000 valedictorians apply to colleges every year. Numbers and rankings will always be important. However, no matter how impressive they are, you still need to distinguish yourself from all the others who look just like you statistically. One panel member stated:

*Clearly, since Ivys regularly deny valedictorians and applicants with 1,600 on the S.A.T., being perfect in those categories isn't as important as other areas. If one thing could be perfect, it should be the essay.*

If you are normally a procrastinator, you need to understand that your success depends entirely on the amount of time and effort you put into the essay writing process. An admissions committee member explained:

*The essay is of primary importance simply because it is the only part of the publication over which the applicant has one hundred percent control. Even a great interview can be discounted if the interviewer is prone to inflate her summary.*

We are not trying to create stress or scare you with this information. On the contrary, this knowledge should motivate you, even if writing is not your strongest area. The essays are more about revealing the personality of the author than they are about showing off any specific skill or achievement. They provide you with a sure way to make a positive impression with your application. You should think of them as a vital opportunity to express yourself, to give your application a face, and to vault yourself from obscurity into the spotlight.

## What Are "They" Looking For?

As we have said before, knowing how important the essays are is half the battle. The other half is understanding what makes an essay good. Whether consciously or not, you probably already have an image in your head of what the committees look for in an applicant. Many students assume that they look for only extreme academics. Therefore, the applicants try to make an impression by cramming their essays full of S.A.T.-type vocabulary quiz words, or they try to sound mature by using a stiff, formal tone. Nothing could be more misguided! In reality, these are exactly the kind of hackneyed essays the committee is tired of reading.

Believe it or not, the activities portion is more important than the awards portion on an application, and it receives more scrutiny. The admissions committee looks for how your activities will translate to their campus. Does your record of activities show that you stick with an interest and follow it through? Do you jump around a lot and show a lack of focus instead? An admissions officer explained:

> *The most important thing for students to realize is that colleges are not just trying to admit people who are smart enough to do the work; they want to admit interesting people who will make a contribution to the incoming class. The biggest mistake that students applying to top colleges make is thinking that good academic credentials are all they need. They do not put much time or effort into listing their extracurricular activities or community involvement because they think it is a waste of time. They are concerned with looking serious, and they are afraid that the admissions committee will see these things as frivolous.*

If the committees are not looking for the superintellectuals, who are they looking for?

## The Real You

To write the best possible essays, all you need to do is show the committee members who you really are. Try to engage them, and aim high. Do not be afraid to take risks. The very best essays are the ones that get a real reaction from the reader. One admissions officer said:

> *I've been moved to tears, awestruck, laughed until I gasped, impressed, and most importantly, educated by many of the applications I've read.*

> *What does presenting a real person actually mean, though? It means that you should BE YOURSELF! One committee member explained:*

*It is through the essay that the admission officers reading the application will feel they have truly gotten to know you. You must develop your own voice and tell YOUR story, not the story you think the reader wants to hear.*

Be completely sincere. If the question asks you about your favorite book, do not write about *Moby Dick* or *The Odyssey* because you think it will make you look smart. Be proud of who you are and what you love, and stop worrying about what the committee will think. If you write sincerely about your true passions, a real person will materialize, and you will capture the committee's interest. If, on the other hand, you present a series of statistics or bore the admissions team with an overly stiff or serious style, you will not endear yourself to them—you will simply make them yawn. Here is how one admissions officer put it:

*Admissions officers tend to have a very emotional, almost romantic, vision of their jobs. They love people, and they love to tell anecdotes about people. They prefer the particular to the general, the specific to the universal, and the anecdote to the abstract (and what reader doesn't?). They are searching for some intangible quality in the application that no number could ever reveal. They hope to find it in the essay. Never squander the chance to tell them who you are in the essay. It helps them to reassure themselves that the process is human and that what they do for a living matters to another human being.*

### Engineers, Computer Jocks, and Other Techie Types

If you are one of the millions of computer jocks out there who assumes that this does not apply to high-tech schools like MIT and Caltech, get ready for a wake-up call. You might be banking on the fact that they will overlook weak essays in lieu of your stellar math abilities. The fact is, though, that you techies have an even greater need to humanize yourselves than your liberal arts counterparts. Listen to what an eight-year admissions veteran who has served at Caltech had to say:

### Applying to Technical Institutions
By Marcey Whaley

*The qualities that prestigious technical institutions such as Caltech or MIT seek in their applicants are very similar to those sought by the best liberal arts colleges. Many students applying to technical institutions have the impression that writing ability, social skills, and extracurricular involvement carry little weight. They think that high S.A.T. or A.C.T. math scores and hours logged in front of a computer are all that matter. Unfortunately, many high school counselors are under the same impression.*

*Nothing could be further from the truth. Remember that technical institutions, like their liberal arts counterparts, are seeking to build a class, a group of people who will live together comfortably, create an interesting and stimulating environment, and contribute to the institution. The image of places like Caltech and MIT as havens for socially inept computer jocks is completely false.*

7

Admissions officers at such places seek students who excel in several different areas. You demonstrate this by having strong S.A.T. and/or A.C.T. scores in science and math, having strong grades in science and math classes, and participating in science- and math-related activities. These include science fairs and competitions, summer science programs, and employment related to science or math. One thing that usually catches the eye of an admissions officer at a technical institution is entry into the Westinghouse Science Competition. Even if you do not win, the time and trouble required for entering the contest attest to a strong interest on your part. Other indications of strong aptitude and ability for science and math are awards such as the Bausch and Lomb at graduation. Admittedly, you must show a strong aptitude for and interest in science, math, or engineering.

In addition to demonstrating your ability in science and math, however, all other aspects of your application must be strong. Grades in humanities and social science classes must be top notch. It is the kiss of death to submit transcripts with uneven grades in these subjects. It is even worse to excuse such grades by claiming to be bored with subjects not related to math or science. You will be expected to take classes in humanities and social sciences no matter which institution you attend. Employers at high-tech companies increasingly search for employees who possess not merely technical skills but strong communication skills as well.

While the personal essay required by technical institutions may not carry as much weight as those submitted to a liberal arts school, I can assure you that your essay is read and reread very carefully. At the very least it must be coherent, with ideas flowing logically from one to another, with correct grammar and absolutely no spelling mistakes. (Do not rely solely on your spell checker. It will not pick up misplaced homonyms like to and too.) The essay is your chance to show the admission officer how you differ from the thousands of other applicants with top scores and grades. What could you bring to the institution that no one else in the applicant pool has? Write with conviction and confidence. Try to add a little humor if you can manage it without being obnoxious!

It is important to establish good relationships with several of your teachers and with your counselor. The admissions committee takes their input very seriously when evaluating applications. An experienced admission officer can spot the difference between a glowing letter written by a teacher who knows you well and a polite but not very detailed note written by someone who has never even spoken to you outside of class.

The area in which applicants to technical institutions are weakest is usually extracurricular activities. Nearly every applicant in the pool has strong test scores and grades and has demonstrated interest and ability in math or science. Those things simply get you past the first cut. The factors that determine who will finally be offered admission are less-easily defined but crucial. The admission committee looks for students who will be able to bring something besides mere intellectual muscle to the entering class. They look for musicians, artists, athletes, and debaters. Student leaders are desirable, but so are those who quietly work behind the scenes to get things done. If you have had interesting travel ex-

*periences, had poetry published, or scored the winning touchdown for your team, you should mention it. If you have done community service, earned the rank of Eagle Scout, or tutored grade-school kids, the committee wants to hear about it. Because of family circumstances you may have had to work a great deal and may not have had time for as many activities as you would have liked. This is important to mention, as well.*

*Technical institutions often receive applications from students whose families discourage involvement in extracurricular activities, believing that the admission committee may regard such activities as frivolous. Such well-meaning parents often demand that their students focus on studies to the exclusion of all other activities. This is unfortunate. When an admission committee sees that a student is able to maintain outstanding grades and become proficient in some other area, it speaks volumes about that student's ability to manage time, maintain priorities, and contribute to the larger community. The committee rarely gives the most serious consideration to students whose applications betray a narrow focus on academics.*

*In short, much of the good advice you read elsewhere in this book about how to create a strong application for admission to a liberal arts institution applies to your application to a technical institution. The most important thing to remember is that admission committees seek to build a class of people who will enjoy spending four years together and who will contribute something to the institution as well.*

## Five Key Attributes

Now that you understand that admissions officers want to find real, live human beings when they look to your essays, it is time to get more specific. We have identified five crucial factors for making your essays come to life. These factors are based on our interviews with top admissions officers around the country. They are listed below.

### 1. Get Personal

The best way to show a committee who you really are is to make your essays personal. When you do this, your essays will automatically be more interesting and engaging, helping you to stand out from the hundreds of others the committee will be reviewing that week. One admissions officer explained:

*Personalize your essays as much as possible—generic essays are not only boring to read, they're a waste of time because they don't tell you anything about the applicant that helps you get to know them better.*

What does it mean to make your essays personal? You must drop the formalities and write about something you find truly meaningful. Include a story or anecdote taken from your life, use lots of details and colorful imagery to give the essays life, and above all, be honest.

All of the top five essays included in Part Four of this book are good examples of

ESSAYS THAT WILL GET YOU INTO COLLEGE

essays that got personal. Essay 31 is perhaps the best example of all: this applicant writes an intensely personal account of growing up gay and Asian. He writes about his first crush, about the alienation he has endured, and about trying to suppress his sexuality. He also writes about his growth and development through all these experiences, how he has changed, and how his identification with the various stereotypes of homosexuality has defined and limited his world. Importantly, he writes using his own voice and on his own terms, referring to himself at one point, for example, as a "crusading warrior princess."

It is very important to note, though, that as one admissions officer put it:

> *A personal epiphany, tragedy, life change, or earth-shattering event is not essential to a strong essay. True, these topics often tug at the heartstrings and therefore get more notice. But I've read essays about a family vacation, a garden, a grandmother—even a pen!—that I've thought have been fabulous. You don't need to be a gay Asian activist to get noticed.*

We cannot stress this enough. Personal does not have to mean heavy, emotional, or even inspiring. Only a small minority of students will truly have had a life-changing event about which to write. Perhaps they have spent time living abroad or have experienced death or disease from close proximity. However, this is the exception, not the rule.

In fact, students who rely too heavily on these weighty experiences are more likely to do themselves an injustice. They often do not think about what has really touched them or interests them because they are preoccupied with the topic they think will impress the committee. They write about their grandfather's death because they think that only death (or the emotional equivalent) is significant enough to make them seem deep and mature. These applicants often rely on the experience itself to speak for them and never explain what it meant to them or give a solid example of how it changed them. In other words, they do not make it personal.

### Poor Jessica

An article by Carey Goldberg that appeared in the December 31, 1997 edition of *The New York Times* examines the perceived difficulties college applicants face when choosing a topic for their admissions essays. It begins with the story of Jessica, then a high school student in Massachusetts. "In her desperation," the article begins, "17-year-old Jessica . . . found herself wishing that somebody—anybody—in her family had died."

"'Because then I could write about it,' she said. 'It's horrible and I hated myself for it. But I just wished I had something tragic happen to me.'"

When Van Sturgeon, the former Associate Director of Admission at Duke University and now the Director of Admissions and College Placement at the South

Carolina School for Science and Mathematics saw this article, he felt he simply had to respond, not just to Jessica, but to all students who believe that they would not be able to produce a good essay without having had something tragic happen to them. He submits the following to anyone who has felt themselves in "poor Jessica's" shoes.

### Mr. Sturgeon's Response

This dismaying article provided the front page headline for the New Year's Eve edition of the *Durham Herald Sun*. What a way to end the year. Poor Jessica. She is making two grievous mistakes. And you are prone to make them, too. So you may want to read this carefully. Her first mistake is assuming that someone else's death would ennoble her. The other is her conviction that she could write effectively about it.

Let's take the second assumption first. Jessica takes it for granted that since death is so extraordinary, her resulting prose would be towering. Sorry, Jessica. Life doesn't work that way. "Listen, Jessica," I would say, "if you can't write forcefully about how to tie your shoelaces, you'll never be able to write convincingly about the tragic, awe-inspiring, terrifying mystery called death. Death has produced more nonsensical, underwhelming, and lurching prose than any topic in history (with perhaps the exception of love.)"

Jessica's "dream" essay about death would be as simpleminded, trite, and inelegant as her comments in this article. Since I have read thousands of college essays, I can tell you exactly what Jessica would have written had she been blessed to have someone she truly cared about swept into the abyss. She would have written the "Permanent Sanctifying Effect" essay. It goes like this: "I had everything. I took it all for granted again." My mother/father/friend/cat/goldfish died. Jessica was looking for some *convenient* way to say, "I was once a thoughtless immature adolescent. I survived a rite of passage. I am now a thoughtful, mature, productive adult. And, oh, by the way, accept me to Harvard." Unfortunately, no one she knew had the decency to die for her educational salvation.

This belief in sanctification by ordeal comes in a variety of packages: death, disaster, divorce, and disease top the list. All of which produce the same hackneyed essay. "I had everything..." It is one of our most well-guarded myths that suffering has a lasting sanctifying effect on us. You know, misery makes us better. No. If someone dies or a hurricane strikes or a river floods a town, people suffer. Rarely does it make us "better." Becoming a "better" person takes daily persistence and commitment, whether or not there is tragedy in our lives.

Snap out of it, Jessica. I hope I've convinced you to forget the death stuff. Now let me ask you this: Why do you want to go to Harvard anyway? To get a high paying job, or for the prestige, or because your parents are needling you (not to death,

11

I hope). Look around you. I mean really look at all the wonderful opportunities that are begging for your attention. LOOK! The author of this article quotes statistics from Harvard, admissions officers from Wellesley, Swarthmore, and William and Mary. The heck with them. As unthinking and banal as you are, Jessica, there are still hundreds of colleges that would be eager to admit you and could perhaps do a better job than Harvard of helping you overcome your shallowness.

Jessica, do you really believe you can get a better education at Harvard than anywhere else? No, you just want the name brand because your beliefs are so superficial that you define yourself by the clothes you wear, the car you drive, the name on your degree, and by who you know that died. If you cared a wit about education, you could never have stooped to wishing for the death of a loved one, no matter how "horrible" you claim it makes you feel. If you cared about anything meaningful, you'd have your topic right there. If you had listened to your English teachers for the last twelve years, and had a thought in your head other than how to get a good grade on the test so you could get into Harvard, you'd know how to write an effective essay.

Learn to think. Hunger to grow. Set some meaningful goals for yourself then pay the price day in and day out to meet those goals. But, most of all, get over yourself.

Read Essay 51 for an example of this. The applicant writes about his mother's bout with cancer. He writes about an experience that undoubtedly must have affected him quite deeply. However, notice the reaction it received from the admissions officers:

*I yearn to know more . . . .*

*Things seem a bit too tidy . . . .*

*It's too easy and convenient to be believable . . . .*

*This essay smells of contrivance . . . .*

*The writing style [is] artificial and a bit maudlin . . . .*

*I don't believe the "epiphany" in the conclusion as it's described . . . .*

What is the real reason this essay flopped? The essayist relied on a personal subject but did not write about it in a personal manner. Essays that do just the opposite—that take a commonplace topic or experience but are personal—are often highly successful. Essay 34 is a good example of this. The applicant writes about catching his first fish at the age of seven. Compare the following comments to the previous ones:

*I get a strong impression of the kind of person this young man must be . . . This could have been another bland essay, but the writer took you on the adventure with him . . . .*

*[The writer] was able to take the experience and make the connection to his life and goals of today. . . .*

*[It] describes vividly and movingly the young boy's first experience with death and with personal responsibility. . . .*

Comparing the different reactions should help you better understand what it means to get personal in your essay. However, it can still be a hard quality to achieve and even harder to recognize in your own writing. One way to gauge the effect of your essays is to have someone objective—preferably someone who does not already know you well—read them over when you have finished. Ask the reader if he or she got a sense of the kind of person you are. If so, that's a good first step but be sure that the qualities the reader uses to describe you are both positive and accurate reflections of who you really are.

### 2. Details, Details, Details

One way to make your essay instantly more personal and interesting is to use plenty of details. An essay without details is like food without flavor. It might fill you up but who wants to eat it? One committee member explained:

*Details provide the color, the spice, and the life of the essays.*

Using detail means getting specific. You need to back up each and every point that you make by specific instances, examples, and scenarios taken from your experience. These details make your story special, unique, and interesting. Look at the detail used by the writer of Essay 37, for example. He is very specific, even from the first sentence. He boarded a plane at "The end of July that took him from "Cincinnati, Ohio, to Nairobi, Kenya." Then he really expands into colorful detail in the third paragraph, describing the "Hippos floating like rocks in Lake Victoria," and the "Flamingos balancing knee-deep in a salt-lake." He didn't just climb a mountain. He "Hiked 17,000 feet above sea level to the peak of Mt. Kenya." This whole paragraph could have easily been boiled down to, "Living in Africa for a year was an unforgettable experience that taught me many things." This is the difference between a fun, interesting treatment of a story and a yawn-inducing account that could be attributed to any of a thousand applicants.

Using detail also means that you back up all your claims and assertions with tangible evidence or descriptions of results. Use actual experiences or even numbers and statistics if you have them. Essayist 41 does this when writing about the success of his bridge club. "Sixteen new students learned how to play bridge; five enjoyed the game so much that they are now frequent players at duplicate games."

Essayist 45, on the other hand, is an example of a good writer with a solid and interesting topic who would have benefited enormously from taking this advice.

In the essay, he focuses on two qualities that make him unique—pragmatism and idealism. However, all he ever really does is assert that he has these qualities. He tells us that he has them, but does not show us. Had he described even a single scenario to back up his claims, the essay would have gone from good to great. As one admissions officer put it:

> Give me one concrete example of a change you've already made. Be genuine enough to give the reader a good-faith deposit on your lofty proclamations. As the saying goes, "If you're gonna talk the talk, you better walk the walk."

Although it is true that the use of excessive detail can bog down the pace of a story, don't even think about limiting the scope of what you incorporate during the first phases of writing. Too much detail in your writing is a much less likely pitfall than the alternative. To begin, err on the side of too much information and you can trim it down later. This way you won't find yourself manufacturing detail to fit neatly into an essay you thought was complete, but that turned out to be less than engaging.

### 3. Be Different/Unique/Interesting/Funny

Being different is easier than you think—after all, you are a unique person. *Showing* you are different is harder, but this is what will make your essay stand out. In order to accomplish this, it pays to take calculated risks. An admissions committee member explained:

> Applicants should not be afraid to go out on a limb and be themselves—even when that means incorporating humor or being a little bit controversial. They are so often afraid of making the correct impression that they edit out anything that would help their essay stand out. They submit a "safe" essay that is, in reality, sterile, monotonous, and deadly boring.

Just as you need not have had an emotional, life-altering experience to make your essay personal, you also do not need to have had an unusual upbringing or background to have an unusual or interesting essay. Do you have any interesting hobbies or passions? Essayist 41, for example, made himself stand out by writing about his unusual passion for playing bridge.

Even if there is not a single thing about yourself that you feel differs markedly from any other student, do not despair. In the end, how you write about your topic will make you interesting and unique, not what you write about. So even if you feel like you have lived an unremarkable life, you can still be creative by coming up with an interesting slant on an ordinary life event. Essayist 35 is the most extreme example of this. She writes about something that all of us do on a daily basis: shower. However, she writes about her topic creatively enough to land her essay in our top five ranking.

We have one word of caution. In an effort to make yourself sound more unique or more interesting, you may be tempted to create an image of yourself that looks great on paper but is not exactly accurate. Being creative and different is great but it is even more important to . . .

### 4. Be Honest!

You should uphold this point without exception. Nothing about the application process could be more simple, more straightforward, or more crucial: be honest, forthright, and sincere. Admissions officers will not tolerate hype. Do not try to create a larger-than-life impression of yourself or worse yet of someone you think the committee would accept. You will be perceived as immature at best and unethical at worst. An admissions officer explained:

> *After 15 years of reading hundreds of essays a year, you develop an amazing ability to see straight through the bull.*

Some of the essayists in this volume go so far in being honest that they admit to weaknesses, mistakes, and other instances that could be seen as drawbacks, even when they are not specifically asked to do so. Essayist 38, for example, wrote, "I must admit that my record was not very impressive. Never before had I completed anything. I played soccer. I quit. I was a Cub Scout. I quit. I played trumpet. I quit. Karate was all I had left." In this case, this approach works because it helps to explain the subsequent drive and ambition he shows when training for his fight. It is also crucial that he demonstrated that he did finally commit to something (karate in this case). That way, he highlights growth rather than failure.

Others admitted to weaknesses less successfully. Essayist 43, for example, wrote, "I admit that I was born a coward." One admissions officer wrote: "If I had been advising the author before he sent in this essay, I might have suggested that he make the tone just a little less self-deprecating. [It]. . . plays against the overall tone of the essay." The admissions officers also noticed that the writer of Essay 40 mentioned having a "Lack of time for academics, due to my involvement in all these exciting activities." Although the essay overall was received well, the writer definitely did not need to bring this up. It made one officer "Hesitate a bit. . . . If her transcripts revealed weak grades, I would seriously doubt her ability to manage her time well enough to keep up with the increased demands of college-level academics."

Being sincere does not mean that you have to admit to your every folly. Drawing attention to negatives is not a requirement of truthfulness—you can be honest and still be completely positive about yourself and your qualifications. Ultimately, it is a very personal decision. If you do call attention—in any way—to your drawbacks, be sure to get plenty of feedback from an objective person before you send your essays in. You should feel confident that you have addressed these weaknesses with finesse and have not weakened your stance.

### 5. Tell a Story

Incorporating a story into your essay can be a great way to make it interesting and enjoyable. The safest and most common method of integrating a story into an essay is to tell the story first. Then step back into the role of narrator and explain why you presented it and what lessons you learned. The reason this method works is that it forces you to begin with the action. It can be tempting to write an introductory paragraph before you begin the story—but resist! These introductions rarely work. Several committee members explained:

*The applicant should never begin an essay with grand proclamations about the nature of man and the universe. Tell a simple story, and let the reader make inferences from it.*

*If the first paragraph doesn't fix my attention, like anyone doing required reading, I'm prone to begin skimming.*

The essay section contains many examples of applicants who have done this well. Essay 34, for example, uses the story of the writer's fishing adventure as the bulk of the essay. The writer steps away from it only in the concluding paragraph, where he explains how the story has affected him and how it ties into his present life. Essayist 32 uses story to a much lesser degree. She sets up her scenario only in the first paragraph. Then once the reader is drawn in, she uses the story as a springboard to discuss the year she spent in Switzerland.

Some writers choose to write the entire essay as a story without ever stepping out of the action. Essay 44, for example, says all it needs to say purely in the context of the hospital visit. The writer literally offers no explanatory text. Most of the admissions officers enjoyed this essay. One "Absolutely loved it," and notes the "smooth transitions" and "crisp imagery." Another, though, remarked, "It doesn't say much of anything!" and it "is sweet, but I don't know quite what to make of it."

If you are not comfortable writing an actual story or piece of action into your essay, you can still add interest by writing your essay to read like a story. One way to do this is to soften the language that you use. Write with your real voice, informally, as though you were telling someone a story. Committee members said:

*Use a conversational style and easy-to-understand language to project a genuine, relaxed image.*

*Make sure that your essay is readable. Don't make us work. Give your essay momentum—make sure the parts work together and move to a point, carrying the reader along.*

Like all advice, though, take this with a grain of salt. Going too far with an informal voice or incorporating humor can rub some committees the wrong way.

They want to know that you take the process seriously. Plus, humor is highly individual—what you find funny might offend an admissions officer. One stated:

> *Humor is a powerful tool, so use it wisely. Gimmicks are a big mistake, and a sarcastic or flippant tone will often offend, but real humor, inventiveness, and dry wit are always in good taste.*

## What They Are Tired of Finding

Not surprisingly, much of what admissions officers are tired of finding is simply the converse of what they hope to receive. In other words, do not try to be something you are not. Do not lie. Do not hand in a poorly written, ill-constructed document riddled with grammatical errors.

Admissions officers cited a few pet peeves so frequently, however, that they bear repeating. After all, they would not be pet peeves if people were not still doing them.

### Don't Be Dull!

One committee member emphasized:

> *Don't bore us! More often it is the monotonous style, and not the subject matter, that makes these essays dull.*

This was by far the number one don't on the list. This pitfall, again, results from the applicant writing for some stereotyped image of what schools want. Even the most interesting or impressive topic can be killed by writing in a dry, academic style. Another admissions officer said:

> *What do I hate? Large words used clumsily. Colorless adjectives and weak verbs. Long lists of activities and accomplishments.*

One way to avoid this trap is to put your thesaurus away. Make it a rule to use it only when a specific word is right on the tip of your tongue but you cannot quite remember what it is. Whatever you do, do not use your thesaurus to find big words that you think will make you sound smarter. Admissions officers pick up on this quickly. One officer commented about Essay 43, for example:

> *I wonder if the word "travails" in the first sentence was actually the first word that came to the author's mind. It sounded immediately to me as though he had checked a thesaurus for a fancier word than "trials" or "problems," and it sounded unnatural and forced. As a rule, try not to use words that you wouldn't use in normal conversation.*

Another pitfall that results in a dull essay is to do little more than list activities, interests, or achievements that can be found elsewhere in your file. One committee member emphasized:

*Listings of anything are dull, no matter how impressive. Save them for the other parts of your application.*

You can write about an award or honor (some questions specifically ask for it), but be sure to reveal something about yourself in the process. Tell a story about what it took to get you there and how it has affected you since. The writer of Essay 54 falls into the list trap and was not received well by any of our admissions officers because of it. "Blah. Tells me little more than I would otherwise get from a list of extracurricular activities," writes one. Another comments:

*This was an "I did this and I did that" type of essay. . . . It seemed to be derived from the student's list of extracurricular activities. Essays should be about more than a running tally of accomplishments. It is obvious that this student is quite intelligent and involved, so I find this attempt at a college essay rather baffling.*

## Mind the Mechanics

You can make no excuse for having typographic or grammatical errors in your essay. These are the types of errors you can easily correct and are costly if you do not. One surprisingly common mistake is forgetting to replace the name of the correct school throughout the essay. Thus, Harvard receives essays each year beginning, "The reason I want to attend Stanford. . . ."

We have listed below a few other common mechanical errors as cited by our admissions team:

*Keep the essays within reasonable length. Excessively long essays show a lack of consideration—we have thousands more like yours to read, and seeing a long one just makes us tired.*

*Don't cram your essay onto the page with a tiny font. If I can't read it without a magnifying glass, I won't read it at all.*

*ACTUALLY ANSWER the question they ask. Many people just list off their accomplishments and never relate it to the theme of the question.*

*Proofread! Have others proofread! Spell check! It's stunning how many people have careless, even really obvious typos in their statements. It makes the applicant look sloppy, uninterested, unintelligent.*

## Get Feedback!

We have mentioned this several times already, but it bears reiteration: It is imperative that you get feedback about your essays before submitting your final versions. For a variety of reasons, many of the don'ts listed above are hard to spot in your own writing. Find an honest, objective person to read the entire essay set for one school. As comforting as it might be, do not accept a simple, "They're great!"

Ask the reader to look specifically for the dos and don'ts listed in this chapter. Ask that person to recount to you the main points you were trying to make. Have him or her describe the impression he or she received about your strengths and weaknesses. Approach the reader a week after that person has read the essays and see what (if anything) has remained memorable. Finally, if the person is not familiar with what a successful admissions essay looks like, have that individual read some of the samples from "The Top Ten" section in the back of the book to have a measuring stick by which to judge your work.

Lastly, do not rely on only one person's opinion, especially if you know the person well or disagree with the points he or she has made. Even the most objective reader has his or her own set of biases and opinions. No one person can accurately predict the reception your writing will have at the school to which you apply.

One way to offset this potential risk is to have one of your evaluations done by a professional. A number of these types of services can be found through your guidance counselor or on the Internet. (See *www.ivyessays.com*.)

## CHAPTER 2

# Gather Your Material

**Chapter Highlights**

Make a comprehensive list of your activities, skills, and accomplishments. (Public recognition for accomplishments is not necessary.)

Using a free-flowing style, write down who you are and what you want.

Identify your personal and professional goals (even if they are broad).

Make a list of all meaningful experiences since childhood.

Note your major influences—people, books, or other sources of inspiration.

Research the schools and be able to demonstrate why they are a good fit for you.

Using a blank page for each question, list each relevant topic that you've identified.

Now that you have a better understanding of your audience and some of their opinions about what makes an essay exceptionally good or bad, you may feel ready to begin writing. You may even feel inspired about a particular topic and have gotten some good ideas for presenting it. Before you turn on your computer, though, stop for a moment and assess your situation.

Creating an essay full of imagery and detail will require you to think carefully about your subject matter before you begin writing. This means much more than simply knowing what your topic will be. It means, first and foremost, that you know yourself. Interesting, reflective, and revealing essays always result from careful self-analysis. It also means that you understand the specific points you wish to make in your essays and have identified concrete details to use in support of each of these points. We often forget the details of our lives over time. Yet these details will provide the material for your essays, making them vibrant and compelling.

This chapter contains a number of brainstorming activities designed to help you get to know yourself better and gather the material you will need to write a colorful essay. We begin with the basics in "Start Your Engines." The exercises in this part will offer solutions to open the channels of your mind and get your pen moving. If you already have lots of ideas for your essays and do not feel the need for a jump start, you might want to skip this section and go straight to "Assess Yourself" and "Research the Schools."

## Start Your Engines

To get the most benefit out of this section, put your anxieties aside. Do not think about what the admissions committee wants. Do not worry about grammar or style. Especially, do not worry about what anyone would think. Worries like these hamper spontaneity and creativity. Focus instead on writing quickly and recording every thought you have the instant you have it. You will know that you are performing these exercises correctly if you are relaxing and having fun.

### The Inventory

This exercise is a launch pad to get your pen moving. The goal is simply to compile an inventory of your activities and accomplishments—school, sports, extracurricular activities, awards, work, and pastimes. You may have already made a similar list during the application process. If so, start with that list and try to add to it. This list will become fodder for topics to use when writing your essays. During this exercise you do not need to write down any qualities, skills, or feelings associated with the activities. For now it is more important to be completely comprehensive in the breadth of topics and items you include. For example, if you taught yourself chess or particularly enjoy occasional chess games with your uncle, you do not need to be in the chess club or have won a trophy to add it to the list. Think of how you spend your time each and every day, and include any items that seem significant to you. Spend no less than twenty minutes writing, and keep going for up to an hour if you can. If you run out of items quickly, don't worry—you will probably come up with more during the other exercises.

### Stream of Consciousness

Take twenty minutes to answer each of the questions: Who are you? and What do you want? Start with whatever comes to mind first, and write without pausing for the entire time. Do not limit yourself to any one area of your life such as the career you wish to have. Just let yourself go, be honest, and have fun. You might be surprised by what kind of results can come from this type of free association.

### Morning Pages

If you have the discipline to practice this technique for a week, you may end up doing it for the rest of your life. Keep paper and a pen at your bedside. Set your alarm clock to ring twenty minutes early. In the morning when you are still in bed and groggy with sleep, start writing. Write about anything that comes to mind as fast as you can, and do not stop until you have filled a page or two.

## Journal Writing

Keep a journal for a few weeks, especially if you are stuck and your brainstorming seems to be going nowhere. Record not what you do each day but your responses and thoughts to each day's experiences.

## Top Ten Favorites

Write down your top ten favorites in the following areas: movies, books, songs, musicians, sports, paintings, historical eras, and famous people. Step back and look at the lists objectively. What do they say about you? Which favorites are you most passionate about? How have these favorites affected your outlook, opinions, or direction?

## Free-Flow Writing

Choose a word from your questions such as *influence, strengths, career, diversity,* or *goals* and brainstorm around it. Set a timer for ten minutes and write without stopping. Write down everything you can think of that relates to the topic, including any single words that come to mind.

## Assess Yourself

We hope that the exercises in the last section successfully stirred your thoughts and animated your pen. If so, then it is time to impose more focus on your brainstorming. These next exercises help you do just that. They concentrate on finding the specific points and details that can be used to answer each of your questions. As you work on them, be sure to retain the open mind and creative attitude with which you approached the last exercises.

First, write down each question you have to answer for every school at the top of a sheet of paper—one question per page. As you work on the upcoming exercises, you will now have all of the questions fresh in your mind as well as a place to jot down items specifically related to each question. For example, as you use the Chronological Method below to uncover experiences throughout your life, you may come across a point or example that seems well suited to answering one of the questions. Make a note of the item on the page with that question, and then go right back to brainstorming. If you can apply one situation or experience to multiple questions, do so. Do not censor yourself. At this stage of the writing process, more is better—we address the techniques of honing in and culling down in Part Two, "Strategy." The objective now is to accumulate multiple items for each question.

## The Chronological Method

Start from childhood and record any and all special or pivotal experiences that you remember. Go from grade to grade and job to job, noting any significant lessons learned, achievements reached, painful moments endured, or obstacles overcome. Also, include your feelings about those occurrences as you remember them. If you are a visual person, it might help to draw a timeline. Do not leave out any significant event.

Because so many questions ask about your past, this exercise can help you uncover material that you will likely use in several places. A few schools will ask you directly about your childhood and have you highlight a memory from your youth. Do not automatically discount memories that you think will seem trite or silly. If an experience from your childhood was meaningful to you, what anyone else thinks does not matter. The writer of the essay below, who was accepted into Princeton, built a wonderfully reflective piece around his recollections of playing in a creek as a child:

## ESSAY 1: Princeton, Childhood Experience

A creek is no place for shoes. I think it's unreasonable to ask children to keep their shoes on in such a place. My bare feet were always covered with calluses from walking down the rough pavement of Peardale Street and around the corner, past the weeping willows, but not as far as the Lindsay's squeaky old swing-set. It was hard to see from the road, and as far as I could tell, nobody ever went there—except for me. Large pines nearby stood tall and erect, looking down at the ripples and currents that nudged each other about playfully, like children in the back seat of a car on a long drive. Stones and pebbles lined the shallow bottom and allowed the water to glide in creative patterns over their smooth surfaces. Larger, moss covered rocks dotted the bank and provided ideal spots for a child to sit and watch and wonder.

The creek often taught me things; it was my mentor. Once I discovered tadpoles in several of the many eddies and stagnant pools that lined the small rivulet. A cupped hand and a cleaned-out mayonnaise jar aided me in clumsily scooping up some of the more slothful individuals. With muddy hands and knees, I set them on the kitchen counter, and watched them daily as they developed into tiny frogs. I was fascinated by what was taking place before my eyes, but new questions constantly puzzled me. Dad was usually responsible for assuaging these curiosities. He told me about different kinds of metamorphosis and how other little tiny creatures lived in the water that I couldn't see without a fancy magnifying glass.

By the creek, my mind was free to wander. I remember sitting silently on a mossy rock and watching the birds; I used to pretend I was one. As my body lay still, my imagination would take flight. High above, looking down on this stream from the pale blue heavens, the wind whistled over my face and the sun warmed my body. When my eyes flickered open, it was usually time to go home. Sometimes I even did.

I was always up for a challenge. My sister and I used to jump from rock to rock, in a kind of improvised hop-scotch obstacle course that tested our balance and agility against one another. She was four years older and I had to practice every morning when she was at school in order to keep up. On the rare occasions that I outdid her, I wore a goofy smirk for the rest of the day.

The creek was a frontier. The stream extended far into the depths of the woods. I thought that if I wandered too far into its darkness, I might be consumed by it and never heard from again. Gradually overcoming my fear, I embarked on expeditions and drafted extensive maps using my father's old compass, a sheet of paper, and a few colored pencils. As my body grew in height and weight, my boundaries grew in extent and breadth.

Years later, I happened to be walking to a friend's house by way of the creek. It occurred to me that what was once an expedition was now merely a shortcut. Although I had left this stream behind, I found others: new questions and freedoms, new challenges and places to explore. But this creek would remain foremost in my memory, whatever stream, river, or ocean I might wade.

You can also use a childhood example to demonstrate a long-standing passion or to emphasize how an aspect of your character is so ingrained that it has been with you since youth. The writer of Essay 1 does this, for example, when explaining his early passion for exploring.

## Assess Your Accomplishments

Write down anything you are proud of doing, no matter how small or insignificant it might seem. Do not limit your achievements to your academic career. If you have overcome a difficult personal obstacle, be sure to list this too. If something is important to you, it speaks volumes about who you are and what makes you tick. Some accomplishments will be obvious, such as any achievement that received public acknowledgment. Others are less so. Many times, the most defining moments of our lives are those we are inclined to dismiss.

The essays included in Part Four of this book demonstrate a wide range of accomplishments, ranging from winning a martial arts competition (Essay 38) to helping a friend with Down's syndrome (Essay 43) to winning a "Grip Test" in gym class (Essay 49). The main thing to remember when brainstorming is not to worry about how big or small the accomplishment is in anyone else's eyes. Simply write down whatever comes to mind, choosing what was personally meaningful to you.

## List Your Skills

Do a similar assessment of your skills. Begin by looking at the accomplishments you listed for the last exercise, and list the skills that these accomplishments demonstrate. When you have a list of words, start brainstorming about specific scenarios that demonstrate these skills. Pretend that you are defending these skills in front of a panel of judges. Stop only when you have proven each point to the best of your ability.

Some of your skills will be obvious, such as artistic, musical, or athletic abilities. Others will be more subtle but just as important! These include the skill that Essay 26 highlights: time management. Writing about this skill works for this applicant because he uses it as a platform to discuss his many extracurricular activities and achievements. Essay 19 is about the writer's leadership skills and dedication. He also uses many examples from his extracurricular activities to back up what he claims. One example says, "Volunteering to help out at a handicapped lock-in at an unfamiliar youth center when no one else wanted to."

## Analyze Personality Traits

Take advantage of the often fuzzy distinction between skills and personality traits. If you are having trouble listing and defending your skills, shift the focus to your qualities and characteristics instead. Make a few columns on a sheet of paper. In the first one, list some adjectives you would use to describe yourself. In the next one, list the words your best friend would use. Use the other columns for other types of people—perhaps one for your favorite teacher and another for family members or classmates.

When you are done, see which words come up the most often. Then group them together and list the different situations in which you have exhibited these characteristics. How effectively can you illustrate or prove that you possess these qualities? Proving your points is important. The writer of Essay 45, for example, wrote about his two defining characteristics: pragmatism and idealism. He chose good qualities. However, his essay would have benefited had he provided better examples of how he has actively demonstrated these qualities.

## Note Major Influences

You can refer back to your "Top Ten Favorites" lists for help getting started with this exercise. Did a particular book or quote make you rethink your life? Did a particular person shape your values and views? Relationships can be good material for an essay, particularly one that challenged you to look at people in a different way. Perhaps you had a wise and generous mentor from whom you learned a great deal. Have you had an experience that changed how you see the world or defines who you are? What details of your life, special achievements, and pivotal events have helped shape you and influence your goals? At this and every stage of brainstorming, do not hesitate to expand and modify lists that you created previously. If at this stage of the process you realize that a strong influence in your life was not in your original list, that doesn't mean it is any less important to you. Add it now. The subconscious mind has an interesting way of retrieving information like this and the brainstorming process is meant to uncover as much of it as possible, in whatever way it surfaces.

Some admissions officers caution against using a parent as an influence, simply because so many applicants do so. However, some of the essayists featured here reference the strong influence their parents have had on them and do it well, such as Essayist 25. The writer of Essay 51 was less successful in mentioning his mother's influence. Other applicants spoke more generally of the family influence, such as the writers of Essays 20 and 55.

Many questions ask specifically about certain influences, such as a favorite teacher (see Essay 17), book (see Essays 11 and 16), or character. However, this exercise can be helpful even if your questions do not specifically ask about these people's influence. If they do, do not worry yet about making final decisions. Let your mind wander free for now, have fun, and list as many possibilities as you can.

## Identify Your Goals

The first step of this exercise is to let loose and write down anything that comes to mind in response to the following questions. What are your wildest dreams? What did you want to be when you were a child? If you could do or be anything right now, regardless of skill, money, or other restrictions, what would it be? Think as broadly as you wish, and do not limit yourself to career goals. Will you have kids? What kind of house will you live in, and what kinds of friends will you have? What would you do if you were so rich that you did not have to work?

Second, play the alternate realities game. Choose your two favorite subjects, and think about the way your life would look in twenty years if you pursued either one as a college major and then a career. Do not worry if you define your career broadly. College admissions committees understand that you will not know exactly what you want to do with your life when they ask questions about your career goals. However, they do want to know that you have at least thought about it—and thought about the role that their school will play in your goals.

If, on the other hand, you do already feel passionate about a particular career, by all means play it up! The writer of Essay 42, for example, has already chosen the unusual career of psychoneuroimmunology. A high school student rarely has such specific and unusual plans. It is certainly not necessary. In fact, had this applicant not sufficiently supported his goal with evidence that he knew about the field (because of his parents' work) and had some personal reasons for choosing it, he would have come across as simply trying to impress the committee—always a huge mistake!

Again, do not forget to brainstorm about your personal goals as well. The writer of Essay 24 seems like she must have had a lot of fun doing this, and it shows. Her essay is interesting and fun to read. It presents her as an imaginative and ambitious person.

## A Note for Everyone Tearing Their Hair Out

If these exercises have proved more than a little difficult for you and you are still struggling to find something worth writing about, it could be a sign that you need to step back and reassess the schools to which you have decided to apply. Truly stubborn writer's block could indicate a number of different problems that you should address before beginning the application process. It could mean, for example, that you are ambivalent about the schools you have chosen. Make sure that the schools are *your* choices and that you are going for *your* reasons. It could also mean that you have not adequately researched your selected schools and are not confident that you have made the correct choices.

The next section, about researching the schools, should help you determine whether you have made appropriate choices or whether you need to go back and do some reassessing. When you feel comfortable with the choices that you have made and confident that you would be happy at each of the schools on your list, then go back to the brainstorming exercises found in this chapter. You should see a big difference in the progress you make!

## Research the Schools

Gathering material about yourself will undoubtedly help you when it comes time to begin writing. Do not forget, though, that you also need to gather material about the school. It is as important for you as it is for your essays that you think about where you are going and why you want to get there. Especially considering that colleges are now receiving more applications than ever, people are being turned away who may be just as qualified as the rest of the entering class but may not seem like the right fit for the school.

Researching the colleges of your choice involves more than a quick skim of the catalogs. Do not underestimate what each school's literature will tell you about them—after all, the admissions officers wrote those catalogs to convey what they consider valuable and unique about themselves. A thorough reading will give you a very good idea of what each school prides itself on, what values and principles they consider important, and what they look for in their student body. Go through the catalogs with a felt-tipped pen and circle all of the significant words and phrases that you find. Often a few key terms show up more frequently than others in a school's catalog. Make a list of these main ideas, then use this list to make connections between yourself and that particular college.

Getting this kind of general sense of a school is a good starting point. However, if you really want to "wow" the admissions committee, you will need to push yourself further. When you have done your research, it shows.

## Admissions Tip: Know the School!

One admissions officer explained:

*I have, on occasion, when speaking to large groups, asked the following: "Will all of you applying to an Ivy League school please stand up." Of course, since I know my audience, I know they will all stand up. "Now, any of you who can name a faculty member at the university it is your dream to attend, remain standing, everyone else sit down." How many do you suppose remain on their feet? Rarely any. My point is that applicants need to move away from abstraction and ground themselves in reality. I have just demonstrated that even the brightest kids applying to the best schools can't provide a simple, direct, and easily attainable piece of information that can set them apart from the rest. In an interview, when asked, "Why do you want to attend," they will offer up some stale recitation from the viewbook or cite the influence of a friend. Never in an interview have I had a student say anything remotely like, "I just read Henry Petroski's book* To Engineer Is Human. *I want so badly to take one of his classes." Ivy faculty are laden with well-known thinkers and writers. Know who they are and use that information to your advantage. You may just learn something really meaningful that you didn't know about your alleged "dream" college in the process.*

The first, and most important, question to ask is Do you know what you want? This section presents a series of issues to consider and is designed to help you determine the most important factors for you. Remember that although you are going to college to learn, you are also going there to live. Think about what will make the next four years comfortable and fun—this is just as important as  what that degree will get you once you have graduated. Every year, hundreds of students get into Ivy League schools and turn them down. They opt instead for schools with less prestigious names that, for whatever personal reasons, seemed to suit them better.

Now get ready to ask yourself some questions. In the following, you will find just a few of the things worth considering when researching schools.

## Location and Size

How far away from home are you willing to go? Consider that if you go too far, you will not be able to visit home very often. Do not neglect to take into account the cost of transportation. Nothing is more depressing than being stuck on an empty campus during a major holiday because you cannot afford to go home. Lastly, what part of the country is the school in, and how much do you know about it? Can you handle a climate change?

Also think about the environment the school is in, whether big city, suburbs, or rural farmland. Small, rural schools mean smaller classes and more personal attention. Big schools mean more activities and cultural opportunities. However, big schools also require you to take more responsibility for your education and living arrangements.

## Outside Influences

Obvious pros and cons come with attending the same school as your high school friends. Some students look forward to getting a fresh start with a clean slate in a place where no one knows where they came from or who they were in high school. Going to college is truly a chance to reinvent yourself. On the other hand, going to a strange place where you know no one can be intimidating. Familiar faces can make the transition more comfortable.

Also—and we hope this is obvious—don't fail to apply to a college simply because your parents don't want you to, and don't apply to a school you have no interest in because they do want you to. Subject all colleges that your parents suggest to the same scrutiny as any other college on your list. The same goes for your guidance counselor. The quality of counselors varies widely. Many are terrific and can be excellent resources. Others are seriously overworked and recommend the same schools over and over. If the counselor does not know you by sight, take the guidance with a grain of salt. When heeding advice, always consider the source.

## The Serious Stuff

You can use the overall reputation of the school, in addition to the average S.A.T.s and G.P.A.s, to get an idea of academic rigor. Do you want to be the academic star on campus? Do you instead want to be challenged in an environment where most of your peers have scored better than you? You probably want a stimulating environment with students whose academic skills and abilities are equal to, but do not significantly exceed, your own.

Also look at things like class size, student-teacher ratios, and faculty prestige. Think of how amazing it would be to take classes taught by your favorite author. Also try to find out if a school places heavy emphasis on faculty research. This can mean that while the faculty is enormously prestigious, you will never see them because you will be taking classes taught by their graduate assistants.

## Cost

Ideally, cost would not be an overriding consideration when choosing where to apply, but we all know that reality can be very different. Luckily, most competitive colleges offer generous financial aid packages, including loans, grants, and work-study programs, to students who cannot afford to pay the full tuition price. Remember, though, that tuition is a jumping-off point for other financial discussions. Do you mind juggling several outside jobs or graduating with a heavy debt? Would it bother you to go to a school where everyone has more money than you do?

## Special Advice for Transfer Students

According to E. Whitney Soule, the Director of Transfer Admission at Connecticut College, knowing the school well can be especially helpful to transfer students.

### Tips for the Transfer Essay

*Transferring from one institution to another is competitive and complicated. Before a student can even think about the details of transferable credit, housing, and financial aid, he or she must get admitted.*

*Like freshmen applicants, transfer students compete for limited space in a college or university. Submitting solid academic credentials is an obvious requirement. However, most institutions will require an essay that explains the student's reasons for transferring. If done well, the essay can be the most powerful and convincing part of a transfer student's application.*

*Admission officers review hundreds, sometimes thousands, of applications every year and have to make decisions quickly based on the information available at the time of review. They will be especially discerning when considering transfer applications. After all, the student has already been through the application and enrollment process once (sometimes twice!), and an admission officer will want to be sure that the next landing is for good.*

*Since it is unlikely that admission officers will have the time to call an applicant for more information, questions often get answered by extrapolating from the information available in the application. Therefore, an applicant must anticipate the questions an admission committee might ask and then answer them in the essay(s).*

*Without exception, transfer students have specific and tangible reasons for wanting to leave one college and attend another. Every admission committee will want an explanation. It is both appropriate and important for the applicant to be able to articulate the reasons for choosing the first school, why that school is no longer the right fit, and why the next school will be better.*

*For example, if a student writes a simple essay explaining that he wants to transfer from University A to College B, "Because College B is smaller and on the east coast," the admission committee may interpret that the student prefers smaller classes, is homesick, prefers an undergraduate majority, and so on. Yet, had the student written a detailed essay about how his original desire to attend a large university in the Midwest was no longer appropriate given his new passion to study marine biology in College B's new science facility, the admission committee would have confidence in the student's motivation to pursue transferring.*

*Naturally, if an applicant's credentials have obvious inconsistencies, the essay will need to address those as well. For one applicant, the problem might have to do with a curious drop in G.P.A. and for another, it may have to do with a switch in major or concentration.*

*Unfortunately, little consistency exists among colleges and universities regarding transfer deadlines, application requirements, admission formulas, and transfer credit evaluation. However, all transfer students will be expected to explain their circumstances and choices, most often through an essay or two. The transfer essay is a student's opportunity to tell it like it is, to get to the nitty-gritty and defend it with confidence.*

E. Whitney Soule
Associate Director of Admission
Director of Transfer Admission
Connecticut College

## PART TWO

# Strategy

By now you should have uncovered plenty of material for your compositions. The next step is to decide how to focus your essays and how to position them in response to the questions you need to answer. If you skip this step and attempt to use everything you have collected without carefully considering the questions, your essays will lack the focus they need to convey something meaningful about you.

This section represents the last steps you will need to take before creating your first drafts. The first chapter, "Choose Your Weapons," presents exercises and advice to help you identify the most important points you need to make whether you need to write one essay or ten. The second chapter, "Plan Your Attack," suggests topic ideas and strategies to answer specific questions using examples of essays that have worked in recent years.

## CHAPTER 3

# Choose Your Weapons

## Chapter Highlights

*Strategy for One Essay:*

For greatest effect, focus your essay on one meaningful area of your life.

Discuss your subject by telling a relevant story that is personal and interesting.

If covering more than one skill, activity, etc., consider a compare-and-contrast approach.

*Strategy for Essay Sets:*

Your essay set should create a cohesive image of who you are.

After deciding which points you want to convey, tailor each to an appropriate question.

Be clear and direct with short essays—this will help you stay within the word restrictions.

Do not allow your essays to contradict each other or become redundant.

Use the same style and voice throughout the essay set.

One of the biggest mistakes college applicants make is to cram their essays full of every detail they have uncovered about themselves. While feeling afraid of leaving out something crucial, some applicants force laundry lists of accomplishments, honors, and significant experiences onto the reader, which (as we know from the first chapter) is one of admissions officers' biggest pet peeves.

You have a wealth of material that is available to you—from your skills and accomplishments to your family background, academic life, extracurricular interests, career development, and professional and personal goals. Therefore, choosing what to use and what to discard can be a difficult and frustrating step. The secret to saying a lot without saying too much is knowing how to focus. All the material you have gathered can be brought together to support just a few of the most important points you want to make. To help you identify your focus, try the exercises below.

## Find Your Focus

What is focus? When we say that your essay needs focus, we mean something other than finding a topic. The topic of your essay is usually provided by the question and is very broadly defined. Examples of topics are your favorite extracurricular activities, your career goals, or your growth and development. A focus is more specific—it could be an event, person, influence, or thought that sheds light on the topic. To understand this better, look at Essay 23 written for Stanford. The writer's topic is himself and how he has changed in the last four years. His focus, though, is his boarding school. He talks about a few specific aspects of the school to demonstrate and highlight his growth. The essay discusses the emphasis on learning, encouragement of community activity, and fostering of respect.

Because topics can be so broad, finding a focus will help your essay make a stronger impact. You can often find the focus of an essay by concentrating on a particular area of your life, such as sports or family life. To get started, try looking back to the material you gathered in the last chapter. See if the items you have listed can be clustered into categories representing the different areas of your life. Your categories might include your academics, extracurricular activities, community and volunteer work, and family experiences. Which category contains the most points? Are they distributed evenly throughout, or is one favored over the rest? Do you feel that the distribution accurately reflects your priorities? If you are lucky, you will have a particular talent, ability, or passion that will make this exercise simple.

Athletes, artists, and musicians are all examples of people who are provided with an obvious area on which to focus. Still, even these students can be reluctant to write about a single aspect of their lives, worried that they will appear one-dimensional. Instead, they may be involved in so many activities that they cannot stand choosing one over another, so they try to write about all of them. Do not fall into this trap. You will more likely produce a mediocre essay by being too broad and general than by providing too much focus. The writer of Essay 24 made this mistake by trying to write about four different interests: math, computers, sports, and volunteering. Because he tried to write about so much, he was not able to do justice to any one of them. The result was that he seemed less interesting than he should have to the admissions officers. Remember that admissions officers do not use the essays to find out everything you have been doing during the past four years—that is the purpose of the rest of the application. They use the essays to get a sense of the kind of person you are and the passion you bring to your activities.

Applicants who chose to focus on the most dominant areas of their lives wrote the following examples.

## ESSAY 2: Princeton, Athlete (football)

I have learned a great many things from participating in varsity football. It has changed my entire outlook on and attitude toward life. Before my freshman year at [high-school], I was shy, had low self-esteem and turned away from seemingly impossible challenges. Football has altered all of these qualities. On the first day of freshman practice, the team warmed up with a game of touch football. The players were split up and the game began. However, during the game, I noticed that I didn't run as hard as I could, nor did I try to evade my defender and get open. The fact of the matter is that I really did not want to be thrown the ball. I didn't want to be the one at fault if I dropped the ball and the play didn't succeed. I did not want the responsibility of helping the team because I was too afraid of making a mistake. That aspect of my character led the first years of my high school life. I refrained from asking questions in class, afraid they might be considered too stupid or dumb by my classmates. All the while, I went to practice and everyday, I went home physically and mentally exhausted.

Yet my apprehension prevailed as I continued to fear getting put in the game in case another player was injured. I was still afraid of making mistakes and getting blamed by screaming coaches and angry teammates. Sometimes these fears came true. During my sophomore season, my position at backup guard led me to play in the varsity games on many occasions. On such occasions, I often made mistakes. Most of the time the mistakes were not significant; they rarely changed the outcome of a play. Yet I received a thorough verbal lashing at practice for the mistakes I had made. These occurrences only compounded my fears of playing. However, I did not always make mistakes. Sometimes I made great plays, for which I was congratulated. Now, as I dawn on my senior year of football and am faced with two starting positions, I feel like a changed person.

Over the years, playing football has taught me what it takes to succeed. From months of tough practices, I have gained a hard work ethic. From my coaches and fellow teammates, I have learned to work well with others in a group, as it is necessary to cooperate with teammates on the playing field. But most important, I have also gained self-confidence. If I fail, it doesn't matter if they mock or ridicule me; I'll just try again and do it better. I realize that it is necessary to risk failure in order to gain success. The coaches have always said before games that nothing is impossible; I know that now. Now, I welcome the challenge. Whether I succeed or fail is irrelevant; it is only important that I have tried and tested myself.

## Comments

The topic of this essay is how the applicant has matured and changed since his freshman year. He focuses on football. One of the strengths of this essay is that it is well organized. The applicant clearly put time into the structure and planning of this essay. He uses the platform of football to discuss and demonstrate his personal growth and development through the high school years. What he could have done better was spend more time describing himself after he made improvements. As it is, he only tells us about his newfound confidence and drive. This essay would have been stronger had he actually shown us, perhaps by including a story or describing an event where his confidence made a difference.

## ESSAY 3: Columbia, Musician (cello)

For some reason, my parents felt the necessity to inundate me at a young age with extracurricular activities. After school, I was always being driven from tennis to violin to swimming to cello to baseball to piano to karate to near craziness! I could have been called the world's busiest kid at the time. From two of the activities, I have reaped the most benefits. Although my cello has been used less frequently than my tennis racquet, the musical instrument creates the most meaningful ideas in my life.

However, my appreciation for playing the cello did not come immediately. From the time I was nine years old until I left for prep school, I detested Sunday. The first day of the week was torturous "cello day": I practiced all morning, had a lesson during the afternoon, and came home in the evening exhausted. But today, I thank austere old Professor [teacher's name] for forcing me to learn the art in music.

With the hectic schedule I have year round, being overwhelmed is not a difficult task. Therefore, I consider playing the cello one of the most rewarding aspects of my life. Very few people have the luxury of being able to absolutely enjoying themselves in the middle of a workday. I can bomb a physics test, and then five minutes later be in heaven. Totally relaxed, I sway back and forth to the rhythm created by my bow and my fingers; both of my arms work in harmony. Eyes closed, I reach the final note and my left hand creates a slow, soothing vibrato—mediocre cello playing at its perfection.

The cello reigns as the supreme instrument in my mind. Whether blusteringly chaotic or lovingly sweet, good cello playing, with its deep, rich tones and fantastically broad range is the epitome of expression. I also have ample opportunity for the other half of art—interpretation. I feel a delight beyond description when listening to Pablo Casals or Yo-Yo Ma. I am able to just sit there and think about my life, and their masterful music can make me feel ebullience or rage. Most importantly, whether I listen to music or play it, I can reflect upon and enjoy life as one special being.

I wish the venerable Professor [teacher's name] could be alive today to hear me play the cello. "With *feeling*," he would always say. Whenever I played a note out of tune, Mr. [teacher's name] would yell at me until I cried. But now, with my newfound love for the cello, even if he screamed in my ear, I would continue to relish my playing and let him go until he became hoarse.

## Comments

This essayist does a clever job of combining his focus on the cello with gentle reminders that he is involved in much more as well. He does this by beginning with brief mention of "tennis . . . violin . . . swimming . . . cello . . . baseball . . . piano . . . karate . . . ." in the second sentence. Then he quickly hones in on the cello alone, making only one additional indirect mention of the "hectic schedule I have year round." He wisely does not go into more detail about the other activities. This single reference is enough, since the admissions officers can easily refer to the rest of the application for more detail on his other involvements. This writer also does a good job of showing his love for the cello by painting a picture of himself playing: "totally relaxed, I sway back and forth to the rhythm created by my bow and my fingers; both of my arms work in harmony. Eyes closed, I reach the final note and my left hand creates a slow, soothing vibrato…" This image is likely to be the one that sticks in admissions officers minds, making him more memorable.

## Dual Interests

Although choosing to focus on only a single area of your life can be very effective, it is not a hard-and-fast rule. If you are equally involved in two activities or interests, you can still write a focused essay by comparing or contrasting the two. Students who did just that wrote the following essays.

## ESSAY 4: Columbia, Athlete and Musician (sailing and bass guitar)
Write a chapter from your autobiography.

Chapter 34: One Memorable Sailing Practice

The sun's glare off the water forces my watery eyes to close even more. Spray leaps over the bow and blocks my vision as it slams into me like hundreds of little pebbles. The salt water has irritated my eyes enough already, but I am only beginning my practice for today. The Buzzards Bay Regatta is only three days away, and I must get comfortable with the boat.

Skimming over the waves on a screaming plane, the boat senses every movement. The boat is like a leaf being blown across a pond. With only the rear end of the hull in the water, I am half flying and concentrate on positioning my weight aft for the most speed. I shuffle my butt half a foot aft and the boat rounds up towards the wind, but I fight the motion off with the helm and regain my original course.

With one hand on the tiller and the other holding the mainsheet, I see that my hands are in the same position when I play my bass guitar. Comparisons between the two mesh together in my mind as I realize the similarities between bass guitar and sailing. I recall the practicing involved in bass and see how sailing requires the same diligence. My thoughts no longer focus on fine tuning my sailing, but they vividly connect bass guitar playing and sailing.

I probe to find out what the essences of sailing and music are. While on the water in a sailboat, I accept the elements as they present themselves to me. Given certain wind and wave conditions, I manipulate the sailboat to attain the best harmony between by boat and its immediate environment. I imagine the sailboat is an extension of my body and plunge, accelerate, and rock with the sea and the wind, as the boat does. Sailing stresses technique because I need proper form to adjust to all of the different combinations to have twelve different notes in the musical alphabet with which to work, and with my technique I manipulate those notes and arrange them to adjust to varied moods I want to express. Again, painstaking technique is emphasized because by body must encompass the bass to attain the pure harmony between my expression and the notes on the instrument. Meticulously, I pluck, pull, and slide my fingers on the strings as I adjust to the countless combinations. Musicians and sailors alike practice their technique to reach perfection, whether it be in the form of the fastest sailboat or the most sonorous melody. Rooted in the same essence, I discover that I draw from the same method to sail and play music.

Seemingly unrelated experiences converge. Bass guitar and sailing do not seem to relate to one another, but I discover the similarities. Linking bass guitar and sailing consummates the understanding of two of my hobbies. I seek the mastery of my sailing, but I realize that I simultaneously increase my understanding of bass playing as well.

My focus shifts from new realizations back to my sailboat, but the waves are turning into ripples as the sun sets. There will not be any more sailing today, but I can now continue practicing with my bass.

## Comments

This writer maintains focus by making the similarities between his two activities the topic of the essay. The detail with which he describes both activities and the depth with which he analyzes their similarities clearly demonstrate the passion that he brings to both.

## ESSAY 5: Emory, Dual Academic Interests (science and humanities)

What are your intellectual interests?

Well, gee. I don't really know.

Let's try to narrow it down. Do you like the sciences or the humanities?

Both.

Come on now. You can't possibly be interested in both. You're going to have to choose one or the other.

How often does a dialogue like this one occur? The challenge of choosing between the sciences and the humanities is one which most find simple, but some find impossible. I can speak for the latter group because my interests lie in both areas. Certainly, each manner of thought has its own strengths and weaknesses, but, joined together, the two can combine to form a very effective and proficient way to handle many issues. My interests in the pure sciences like chemistry, biology, physics, and higher mathematics are a reflection of my ability and tendency to think logically and to use deductive reasoning to solve problems. At the same time, I cannot rightfully call myself a pure scientist. Knowledge without effect expression is useless, and I recognize the importance of eloquence and language. I truly enjoy the art forms of writing and acting, and history also is very important to me. I find that, coupled together, the humanities and sciences allow me to take the most out of life's experiences, and to tackle problems very efficiently.

I possess an insatiable curiosity about how and why things happen. My quest for explanations has often led me to the study of science. While mathematics, physics, and biology oftentimes serve me with answers to my questions, I also enjoy chemistry. Chemistry, because of its

41

mysterious nature and largely theoretical foundation, is very thought-stimulating for me. It offers the opportunity to use creativity to solve open-ended problems like energy crises, bio-chemical diseases, and engineering dilemmas. I suppose that my interest in the sciences is a result of my tendency to think analytically, rather than the converse. Regardless, I find that science can provide me with the answers to some of my intellectual inquests as well as providing me with a useful tool with which to solve problems, a refined method of thinking.

While I find many answers in the study of the sciences, many remain unanswered. History, English, and the arts fill the void left by the sciences. The study of history is very interesting to me because of its capacity to contribute substance and meaning to the world in which I live. The two months I spent studying in Israel this past summer offered me explanation for some of the Jewish traditions which my family observes, and it also lent me something more. History is an important part of my life, for it gives me a sense of identity and one of belonging to something much larger than myself, be it a religion, a nationality, or a race. By the same account, literature, writing, and art also present opportunities for personal introspect, contemplation, and expression. As a whole, the humanities offer me a way to be a complete person who can take answers to questions, and weigh them for personal value.

The combination of the sciences and the humanities forms the structure of my intellectual being. My thoughts are not idle intangibles, however. I use my method of thinking deductively and logically, as well as my sense of self to accomplish many of my goals. As three-year class president, I have found my place as a leader who likes to help people realize their goals. I have experienced great success in approaching the issues facing me in the scientific manner of analytical thinking and deductive reasoning. The same approach is generally efficient in other activities in which I am involved. I am an active peer counselor and tutor; instances in which good expression is as important as accuracy. Prevention Players, an improvisational drama troupe serving the community's need for education by powerful presentation, is another activity which merges knowledge of social issues with the arts and humanities. Because of my interests in both sciences and arts, I find all of these activities to be very rewarding and enjoyable. My intellectual interests actively shape my character and personality, as well as guide my life in rewarding directions. The sum of every one of these factors gives my life meaning and will hopefully lead me to a place in the future where I can find intellectual stimulation in all of my areas of interest.

**Comments**

This essay addresses a common consternation among college applicants. You might feel pressure to market yourself as either a science or humanities person, and, in truth, this has merit. However, the vast majority of students do not know yet what they will major in—and that is O.K. too. This essayist tackles his own ambivalence head-on. By showing that he has given a lot of thought to his options and to all the areas of study he mentions, this essay works. Also, the conversational tone of the first few lines effectively gets the reader's attention and interest. This is a good example of why students with multiple interests do not need to worry about appearing scattered as long as they write with depth and introspection.

## Your Personal Points

Do not worry if you did not find an immediate focus for your essay. You do not need to be a varsity athlete or violin virtuoso to have a good topic. Plenty of other possibilities exist. You can, for instance, focus on a skill, personality trait, influence, event, or scenario. To help find that focus, look again over the results of last chapter's brainstorming exercises. Start highlighting words, ideas, phrases, and points that stand out or are especially meaningful to you. Then separate these favorites into columns of skills, traits, interests, activities, events, and influences. Patterns should begin to emerge. Do your different columns reflect and support any general tendencies? Can you draw relationships from the skills to the activities to the events?

Say, for example, that your top skill is leadership. Does one of the activities you have listed support this, such as involvement in student government? Does a specific event demonstrate this involvement, like a hard-won election? If so, in your essay you can demonstrate your leadership skills and your extracurricular involvement by telling the story of the election. Essayist 52 does exactly this. If you can find strong connections, ideas for essay topics will eventually present themselves. Your points may not fall into such neat patterns right away—just keep fiddling with your material and brainstorming until something begins to emerge.

The advantage of this strategy is that it gives you more freedom to tailor your essay to the question. Examples of a variety of different focus areas can be found in the next chapter, "Plan Your Attack," along with tips and advice for tackling some of the different question types.

## Working with Sets of Essays

Some schools require you to write answers to a series of questions rather than submit a single personal statement. If this occurs, then you will need to consider the impact that your essay set will have in its entirety. You need, in other words, to put as much thought and planning into the structure, balance, and content of your set as you do into each of your separate essays.

Working with multiple essays has many advantages. First, more essays mean more opportunity to sell yourself to the committee. Second, you do not need to worry about having to cram too many points into one essay or having to leave something out. Multiple essays give you ample space to do justice to all the different areas of your life. Third, because you have the chance to present many different sides of yourself, you can be more creative and take riskier approaches with one of them, knowing that the other essays will back you up if your approach does not go over well with all of the readers.

### Essay Set Strategy

Making an impact with multiple essays requires that you plan and strategize for the set just as you would if you were preparing a single composition. Begin by making two lists. One should cover all the points that you would like to make about yourself. The second should include all the different areas of your life about which you would like the committee to know. Your first list might include skills or personality traits such as perseverance, dedication, or enthusiasm. The second will include some of the topics discussed in the last section such as your extracurricular involvements, international experience, or academic interests.

When you have finished, look at your questions and begin thinking about which ones you can use to convey which points and areas. Picture your essay set as a jigsaw puzzle. Each essay provides a different piece of the puzzle that, when read together, form a single, cohesive image.

Do not be afraid to be creative when it comes to fitting the different areas of your life into the framework of the questions as long as you answer the questions asked. You could use a question about your accomplishments to discuss your diving trophy, for example. Then surprise the committee members by focusing on your love of traveling in answer to a question about extracurriculars.

### Tips for Answering Short Essays

When you are required to answer multiple questions, the schools usually impose a strict word limit for the answer. These questions generally need more attention than longer essays. It is harder to succinctly convey ideas than to ramble on until you have conveyed everything on your mind. The best way to approach them is to write a regular, full-length essay and cut. Begin by reducing the introduction and the conclusion from one paragraph to one sentence each. Choose only the clearest, most direct parts. This is a very effective method for writing anything. You should always let yourself continue to write as long as you are inspired. Do not worry about time limits or length constraints. After you have the ideas on paper, you can go back and look for the pieces of gold buried under all the words.

Some short-answer questions ask for lists of activities, summer work, jobs, honors, reading, and so on. You can take either of two approaches to answer this type of question: the list or the paragraph. For each method, provide complete information about the items you list. If there are multiple short-answer questions on an application, be consistent and use the same method (either list or paragraph) for all answers. Be sure to include the activity, your involvement, and the time commitment. Make it clear that your activities have involved responsibility and effort. Do not worry about the number of activities you list—when it comes to quantity, less is often more if you show true commitment to those few that you choose.

## ESSAY 6: Georgetown, Saudi International Relations

For many years, I have been interested in studying international relations. My interest in pursuing this field stems from several factors which have affected me. First, I have been exposed to international affairs throughout my life. With my father and two of my brothers in the Saudi Foreign Service, I have grown up under the shadow of international affairs. Second, I am fascinated by history, economics, and diplomacy. I believe, through the study of international relations, I can effectively satisfy my curiosity in these fields. A third factor which has affected my interest in international relations is patriotism. Through the Foreign Service, I would not only have the opportunity to serve my country, but also have the chance to help bridge gaps between my country and others. Finally, as a Saudi living abroad, I have been bridging cultures throughout my life. This experience has taught me to look for differences to compromise and similarities to synthesize in order to balance different cultures. In short, I believe that my experiences in life, combined with a rigorous academic education, will enable me to pursue a successful career in the Saudi Foreign Service.

## ESSAY 7: Georgetown, Favorite Class

At St. Albans, especially in our later years, we are given the freedom to choose from a vast array of classes. Using this freedom, I have selected classes which have personal significance to me, regardless of difficulty or appearance on my transcript. However, from these classes, one holds an extraordinary amount of value to me. This course is A.P. Omnibus History, a combination of American and European history. There are several reasons for my great interest in this class. First, I am fascinated by the cyclical nature of the past. I see these recurring political, economic, and social trends as a means of looking forward into the future, while allowing us to avoid the mistakes of the past. Second, history teaches many lessons about the nature of human behavior, both past and present, providing insight into the actions, desires, and aspirations of those around me. Finally, it lays a solid foundation for several disciplines, including political science, economics, and international relations, three fields of great interest to me.

## ESSAY 8: Georgetown, Visual Arts

Another major interest of mine, which I have not had the opportunity to express elsewhere on my application, is the visual arts. Throughout high school, I have used a variety of media to express myself. I began with black and white photography, focusing on the presence of lines and balance in nature. For my work in this medium, I received an award at the St. Albans School Art Show. From photography, I moved on to glass etching. Using a sandblaster to etch the glass, I again concentrated on lines and balance in my works. Moreover, by arranging several glass panes into a sculpture, I moved my study into three dimensions, winning another Art Show award. Currently, I am working on canvas, using oil and acrylic in a Mondrian style, which is based on lines and balance. Eventually, I hope to explore the effects of combining these and other media, creating my own style of artistic expression.

## ESSAY 9: Georgetown, Wrestling

In the past four years of my life, no activity has affected me more than wrestling. Four years of varsity wrestling and the honor of being a team captain has instilled many qualities in me. First, through years of hard work and continuous dieting, wrestling has given me discipline. This discipline has spread to other parts of my personality, including my moral character, work ethic, and preserverence. Another quality wrestling has given me is leadership. As a team captain, I have learned to lead by example, both on and off the mat. Above all, though, wrestling has given me a love of life. Through this sport, I have experienced pain, sacrifice, adversity, and success. Exposure to these feelings—which are, in my opinion, the essence of being—has allowed me to truly appreciate life. I hope to continue wrestling at Georgetown.

## Comments

What immediately strikes the reader about this set—before even reading it—is the balance between the essays. Each answer contains only one paragraph, each of approximately equal length. The solid structure of each essay and the focus of each reflects this outward balance. Each one focuses on a completely different area of its writer's life, another striking detail. The first focuses on his career goals, the second on his interest in history, the third on his interest in the visual arts, and the fourth on wrestling. This is a perfect example of the jigsaw puzzle approach. When put together, you have a well-rounded individual with passion, depth, and involvement in many different areas.

## ESSAY 10: Duke, Sports/Debate

Throughout my life, I have tried to be a well-balanced person. Growing up in the South, I had a hard time fighting the stereotypical image of a Chinese person. I was expected to be a math and science genius and nothing more. As it turned out, I defied my detractors by excelling in English and history along with math and science. And over the years, I have continued to maintain my academic standards.

Nevertheless, I have also made sure that I am more than an academic person. I am an active one as well. In middle school, the most popular game during lunch was a basketball game called Salt and Pepper (white vs. black). The first day of school, I stepped onto the basketball courts and was greeted by cries of consternation, "Who is he? Is he salt or pepper?" But after the game, I had made a name for myself. From then onward, I would be known as Spice, and the game we played became Salt, Pepper, and Spice.

When I moved to California, things were no different. I continued to play an active part both academically and socially. My involvement with Cross-country, Speech and Debate, Ultimate Frisbee and numerous clubs guaranteed that I would not be only known as an Honors student.

Like myself, Duke is much more than an academic institution; it is a living institution. I feel that I will be given the opportunity to excel both academically and socially. Duke is a university known for its rich history and strong academic program. And, at the same time, it is also known for its innovation and progressiveness. These are qualities which draw me to the college.

In addition, Duke and I have a lot in common. The two most important extracurricular activities I have are a major part of Duke University. Duke's Speech team is known for its strong Extemp squad. I remember the time when my speech coach asked me what schools I was applying to. When I had listed my top five choices, he frowned at me and said, "Out of all those schools, I will only respect you if you either join us at Berkeley or go to Duke and extemp." I hope I will be given the opportunity to contribute my part in the Duke Speech team.

Equally important, the Duke University has a well-known Ultimate Frisbee team. I look forward expectantly to becoming a part of the team. Strange as it seems, Ultimate Frisbee is one of my top criteria for choosing my future college. It delights me that Duke places such great emphasis on the two extracurricular activities that mean most to me.

My first year at Duke should be a great one. Majoring in economics at Duke should allow me to both pursue my major studies and allow me time for personal interests in Chinese and the Humanities. Moreover, in my spare time, I plan to join the Speech team and the Ultimate Frisbee team. Hopefully, with my previous experience, I will have an early start in both Speech and Ultimate. Yet, I will never forget why I'm in college in the first place. As long as I give organic chemistry a wide berth, I should be able to continue my level of academic excellence. Overall, my first year at Duke promises to be exciting, if a bit hectic.

## ESSAY 11: Duke, Books

I find Hermann Hesse's book, *Narcissus and Goldmund*, intellectually exciting. After reading the book last year, I remember putting it down and sighing contentedly. I had, after a sleepless night, finally finished. What I reveled in was not the fact that I could sleep, but that I had come away with an inexplicable something. It was not an understanding which could be pinpointed and explained. Rather, it was a sense I felt in the depths of my soul. And yet, what delighted me more was that I knew that I had only begun to understand the book; that there remained countless messages which I could only sense but not grasp. Here, finally, I had a book which could be re-read. And every time I finished, I would come away with a new understanding of something I could not put into words.

Unlike the normal academic, I do not want to find the final answer for everything. Throughout my life, I have always felt a sense of loss after succeeding in a long search. For me, it is not the ends I seek, but the means themselves. I am perfectly content to never find the final answer as long as I will always be able to find a better one.

## ESSAY 12: Duke, Chinese Culture/Economics

Born in Taiwan, I came to the United States when I was five. Armed with only two words ("hello" and "popcorn"), I braved the uncertainties of a complex, new environment. Twelve years later, my vocabulary is considerably larger and I have adapted well to my surroundings. At the same time, I have neither forgotten my native culture nor its language.

My ties with my native Chinese culture remain as strong as ever. I visit my relatives in Taiwan regularly almost every summer and have traveled throughout China. And to everyone's continuing surprise, I have yet to forget how to speak Mandarin. Nevertheless, twelve years in America has made its impressions upon me as well. I am as "American" as anyone my age. The songs I listen to, the sports I play, and the way I speak are all a reflection of that. In short, I am a combination of both East and West.

Nevertheless, I sometimes wonder whether speaking Chinese at home and visits in the summer are enough to maintain my ties with my native culture. Often, when I see my parents reading old Chinese literature or poetry, I feel that I am only in touch with half of what I am. This sense of loss has led me to seek out my old roots. I turn to the East to rediscover what I have lost.

Yet, I cannot resign myself to merely studying my own culture and language. I want to be able to apply my knowledge as well. To me, pursuing a career in business is a very pragmatic solution to my future welfare. My father is a businessman in Taiwan and I have had numerous opportunities to watch him work. Through him, I have discovered my own interests in the business field. I find the way business operates in the East to be very exciting. At the same time, my father has soothed my sense of morality by showing me that it is possible to be an honest businessman in Asia.

Before I learned about Duke, I had made up my mind to study economics and to ultimately pursue a career in international business. I had come to see this path as the best combination for fulfilling both my aspirations towards knowledge and my pragmatic goals of a future livelihood. China, my planned area of focus, is an expanding market with a dearth of skilled business professionals. But I had misgivings because I wanted a school with a strong focus on the humanities as well.

Thus, I find Duke University exciting and perfect for me. It gives me a strong economics curriculum, but still allows me to pursue my interests in the humanities. With economics at Duke University, I will have access to a wide array of studies both within and beyond my chosen major. I will have an edge in the business world by virtue of Duke

After attending Duke (if I am accepted, of course), I will have a clear path before me. My studies at Duke should virtually guarantee me for any graduate business school. And, after my graduate studies, I will be able to realize my dreams. Perhaps, I will be able to serve as a bridge between East and West.

## Comments

These three well-written essays create a strong set. The first and the last would have been impressive on their own. Reading them all together magnifies their impact considerably. This student does an especially good job of targeting the school. This student focuses his first essay on his extracurriculars and relates them to why Duke would be perfect for him. He focuses the third on his Chinese background and how it relates to his career goals and academic interests. Then he also relates these interests to why Duke matches him perfectly. His favorite book provided the focus of the second essay. What makes this second essay better than others like it is that the applicant manages to put himself into the question. He does not just talk about the book, he uses it to talk about himself and stresses the inquisitive nature of his personality—always a plus.

## ESSAY 13: Dartmouth, Debate

Participating in my high school's debate program has been my most meaningful activity these past four years. I have learned how to speak in front of a crowd without becoming nervous, how to think on my feet, and how to argue the merits of any side of an issue. Being on the debate team also allows me to educate myself on current topics of global importance such as the homeless problem, health care, and pollution.

Throughout the three years I have dedicated to the activity, (high school) has always maintained a successful squad and I am quite proud to know that I have earned many of the trophies and awards that have helped make the program so successful and [high school] well known on the debate circuit.

Because of the activity, I have learned that from education to communication, from argument to enlightenment, debate is necessary for two or more humans to transcend mere exchange of thought and achieve synergy instead. I now view success in debate as far more than a trophy; I now see it as evidence that I can successfully communicate my beliefs to others and have them logically accept them as their own, thus priming me for any future challenges involving human interaction.

## ESSAY 14: Dartmouth, Honors and Awards

My most important honors since tenth grade have been winning the Brown University Book Award for my skills in English, being named as a National Merit Semifinalist (Finalist status pending), winning the Journalism Education Association National Write-off Award of Excellence in the Editorial division at a national conference, being selected as a Semi-finalist in the NCTE Writing Contest for my work in prose, being named as an Illinois State Scholar for my academic achievement in high school and my high A.C.T. scores, being selected to the Spanish Honor Society for my consistent success with the language in the classroom, being selected as the Student of the Month in the Foreign Language/Social Sciences division two years in a row for my success in those classes, and in a culminating event, being featured in *Who's Who Among American High School Students* for my overall scholastic success.

## ESSAY 15: Dartmouth, Summer at Dartmouth

Most of my past summer was spent away from home. In that brief month in which I remained in [town name] I worked at [job] in order to earn the money I was going to spend on my trips. My first excursion was to the east coast where I visited several schools and took in the atmosphere of an area to which my midwestern self was somewhat unaccustomed. One school I was considering that I did not visit was Dartmouth. After all, I spent a month there later in the summer. As a participant of the Dartmouth Debate Institute I spent a lot of time in Feldberg, Dana, and Baker libraries; resided in the well-known Choates; attended sessions in Silsby; and dined in the Full-Fare section of Thayer. There was also time for recreational activities such as rope swinging, volleyball, frisbee, sleep (every little bit was cherished), and beautiful hikes up to Dana. I did manage to sit down and work in such a clean, open environment, however. The instructors made sure of that. The four-week institute honed my skills in speaking, researching, structuring arguments, and thinking. As a result, my partner and I were able to break into the elimination rounds at the institute-ending tournament which included the top debaters in the nation. Aside from the debate skills I learned, I found the institute very favorable because of the exchange of ideas taking place between the students and staff. What I learned from those exchanges enlightened me not only as a debater but also as a person.

Although I enjoy all of my subjects, I regard classes I have taken in the social sciences to be the most meaningful. Whereas some classes use formulas to describe natural occurrences, the social sciences show that not everything is explicable in such a clear-cut manner. The social sciences describe people; they describe the people who make up the formulas and how and why that was done. The social sciences also explain the past so as a society, people can avoid past catastrophes and build upon past successes. Not only do they describe how we act as we do, but why we act as we do.

I am not a student who always likes to follow someone else's rules. While most subjects allow for free thought, the social sciences encourage innovative thinking. Those classes expect students to explain why something happened based on certain conditions. I didn't learn that the Iron Curtain was an economic measure in any math class.

As a student my ultimate goal is to understand things. I feel the best way to understand is not by reciting another's thought, but by formulating my own and debating it with people who disagree with me. I believe that exchange of thought is vital in every curriculum, but the social sciences do the most to promote that exchange. I highly doubt that anyone will be debating Einstein's ideas in the near future—and be right.

## Comments

This essayist dedicates the first essay to his involvement in debating. He manages to communicate quite a lot in a short amount of space (what he has learned, what he has achieved, and what debating means to him) without ever losing his focus. The second essay is an example of an answer to a list question ("List your honors and awards"). The third gets more personal by describing the summer he spent at Dartmouth. The strength of this essay is that he sells himself on his knowledge and familiarity of the school. The weakness of this essay is that he tries to do too much and loses his focus after the second paragraph. The conclusion does not seem to fit with the points he has made in the essay—the last line in particular seems to grasp at a clever way to end the piece and it fails.

## ESSAY 16: Harvard, Favorite Books

The novel *Black Like Me* was the most stimulating book I have recently read. I was taken aback by the cruelty the narrator experienced when he was black compared to the hospitality he found as a white man. Possessing the same occupation, clothing, wealth, speech, and identity did not matter when his skin was another color. Given that this was a non-fictional piece, my reaction was even stronger. The book made me favor equality of opportunity for all in every endeavor so others' opinions of them are based on performance, not preconceptions.

## ESSAY 17: Harvard, Favorite Teacher

I selected Mr. [name] because he taught me more than U.S. History; he taught me how to think independently. This wasn't done only to prepare me for the free-response section of the A.P. test, either. I know he did it to make his students responsible citizens and responsible adults. From the outset, he wanted to make sure that we knew how we stood in our political philosophy: strict constructionists or loose constructionists. He wanted to make sure that we didn't gravitate towards empty categories like liberal or conservative, but rather focused on issues separately whenever we needed to take a stand on them. Imagine my surprise when I, the son of two very conservative parents who constantly bombarded me with their rhetoric, discovered that I had strong liberal tendencies on some issues. Aside from political affiliations, Mr. [name] taught us how to make sense out of history by trying to understand the personal motives that went in to any chain of historical occurrences. In his class, I came to the realization that history isn't only a series of names and dates printed in a textbook, but a more complex subject that requires deep thought and analysis for full comprehension. Because of Mr. [name], history is now my favorite subject. He has also been a motivating force outside of the classroom. He always had faith in my ability and constantly encouraged me to do my best. I believe he respected my abilities and wanted to see them developed further. In fact, had it not been for his faith in me, I would have never applied to Harvard, the school I plan to attend in the fall.

## ESSAY 18: Harvard, the "Grip Test"
**(also featured as Essay 49 in the graded essay section)**

It's not that I'm a weak guy, just that I had been somewhat self-conscious about my strength early on in my high school career. My gym class didn't help too much, either. Thanks to a demeaning test of strength appropriately dubbed the "Grip Test," once each quarter I was provided the opportunity to squeeze a gadget, get a score, and have my teacher announce it out loud, no matter how high or (as in my case) how low it was. No matter how hard I tried, the cruel and callous scale never registered above 40. Almost every other male in the class could boast of a high-40's or mid-50's score. I hated that test with a passion. Until recently. When this semester rolled around and I had the gripper placed in my palm, I was prepared for the same old same old. I had been improving slightly from quarter to quarter, but nothing impressive ever happened. I drew in a deep breath, squeezed, looked at the scale, and almost fainted. Sixty-six! In a way only a teenager can appreciate, for an accomplishment only a teenager would find meaningful, I thought

I was in heaven. My success was even sweeter as I watched jocks pale in comparison when they took the test. Sure, to some people my academic accomplishments seem fairly impressive, and I would agree. Yet the grip test situation was much more personal and represented success in an area I normally don't pay attention to. Plus I learned two things. One: I can pride myself on the smallest triviality. Two: I'm glad we don't measure strength in our gym classes with the bench press.

## ESSAY 19: Harvard, Leadership Through Dedication

To me, leadership does not necessarily mean accumulating as many titles as possible in school activities; I feel one leads through his dedication, actions, and contributions. I have always tried to lead in almost everything I set out to do. I feel I have been successful at that. Superficially, I have earned such titles as president of the National Honor Society chapter at my school, Editor-in-Chief, columnist, Investigative Editor, and Editorial Editor of the school newspaper, senior varsity leader in debate, and a Class Representative for Student Council. However, those titles don't begin to tell the story of my abilities as a leader. They don't reveal how I volunteered to help out at a handicapped lock-in at an unfamiliar youth center when no one else wanted to, they don't reveal how I always sought to be on time for work and to avoid boondoggling, they don't reveal how I aided younger debaters with their argumentation so they can have the same success I was lucky enough to enjoy, they don't reveal how I became a role model for the JETS squad by studying my material often, eventually becoming the most medaled member on the team, and they don't reveal all the effort I put into learning my lines and acquiring a good stage presence for Images, my first stage production ever, so I wouldn't single-handedly jeopardize the whole show with my lack of experience. All those actions stress the quality I feel is most important in a leader, dedication. With dedication comes hard work and the ability to seek out solutions when problems get in the way, whether they are with a news page layout or in a student's diction. Because of this dedication, taking charge is second nature for me. People are always willing to follow one with a clear sense of direction.

## ESSAY 20: Harvard, Close-knit Family

I don't view my important characteristics as different from those my family has imparted on me throughout the years. The pride, care, dedication, effort, and hard-working attitude that I view as critical to any success I may achieve have all descended upon me courtesy of my close-knit, Italian family.

Born the child of two immigrants who came here with nothing, only one possessing a college degree, the importance of a good work ethic was stressed by my parents from day one. Through their actions in their jobs and through the verbal lessons on life I began to get from the moment I could communicate, they set an example for me to follow, one of being proud of what I do, no matter what it was, and above all, to care about everything I do as if everything had a big impact. This meant that everything had to be done right and be done well. Undoubtedly, following their own advice carried my parents from their status as blue-collar immigrants who labored as a factory workers to white-collar citizens, one of whom owns his own business while the other works as a bank officer. Those ascensions from nothing only served as other examples for me to follow, examples that delineated the ability for a person to improve through effort.

Another quotation from my father propelled me from the time I started school to today: "No matter what you do, you have to be the best." This set up the inner drive that motivates all my actions. It was what forced me to try hard in school although I didn't know English well enough to always understand the teacher. It's the reason why I have developed my skills. It accounts for my dedication to all activities, and to the hard work I put into all of them as I strive to lead both in class and out. Essentially, my parentage was the first quality that distinguished me as a leader.

Despite all the talk of being a leader, I have never lost sight of the importance of my family. I know I owe my family everything, and as a result, I'll always be close with it.

## ESSAY 21: Harvard, Fun

I pursue a variety of activities for fun and relaxation. I enjoy reading books and magazines (my tastes range from *Time* to *Gentlemen's Quarterly*) on a regular basis, imitating Beavis and Butt-head, and most of all, spending time with my friends. Although I am fan of playing pick-up games of basketball, football, and roller hockey, the phrase "doing nothing with my time" doesn't bother me since I can have a good time just hanging around. I think people, not places, make for a good time.

## ESSAY 22: Harvard, Social Concerns

My major social concerns all revolve around the future. In other words, I'm concerned about what prevents people from rising above their disadvantages. Specifically, I am most concerned with the handicapped, education, and crime.

I feel society's response to handicaps is what really hampers the potential of the disabled. It is important for the disabled to get a better sense of worth and to be able to adapt to, and survive in, today's world. Through National Honor Society (NHS), I have done just that. I have helped out at a lock-in that was designed to foster interaction among the children of the organization, as well as at Special Olympics, where the children participate in sports on a competitive basis so their talents and abilities can be recognized. Whenever the disabled can be successful at an activity, the barrier between them and the rest of society is drastically reduced.

Education is key to other problems such as gangs, drugs, and crime because it can prevent and eliminate them. I try to get students in our school to maximize their opportunities by using the educational resources available. By setting up a tutoring program through NHS, I have matched up needy students with other students who can assist them with their problems in classes. More directly, I help students out with English and show them how to use the Writing Center Lab, an indispensable resource for English students at any level. The more educated a person is, I believe, the more able he is to be successful in the future.

I have dealt with criminal problems in my school by discussing solutions to gangs and other crime in the Student Advisory Committee. We have drafted several proposals to help reduce those problems in our school.

Educating people about such social concerns is also very crucial because they won't fix what they don't think is broken. That is one objective of our newspaper, in which we have written various editorials and news stories to educate the student body on social topics. Through debate, I myself have become knowledgeable on such topics as the homeless, poverty, health care, and the environment. That way I can practice what I preach.

## Comments

Harvard is notorious for its long list of essay questions, as you can see from the seven essays this applicant had to write. The first essay is a standard favorite book essay. His second, about his favorite teacher, goes into more depth and reveals more about the candidate, that he enjoys learning, admires independent thought, and plans to study history.

The third essay in this set (featured also as Essay 49 in our graded essay section) stands out from the rest. Had the panel who graded the compositions understood the context of this essay in light of the six others in the set, they probably would have given it more credit. Its strength lies in its funny, lighthearted approach—it shows a completely different aspect of the candidate's personality. Without it, he would have appeared deadpan serious and probably a bit dull. However, showing the wittier side of himself strengthens the set considerably. It is a good example of allowing yourself to take a risk in one essay, as long as more serious approaches in the others balance it.

## Before You Move On . . .

We have stressed in numerous places throughout this book the importance of proofing your essays and getting feedback. Athough most applicants are stringent about taking this step after writing individual essays, some forget to apply the same advice to their essay set as a whole. Before you send in your application, be sure to assess the impression your essays will make when taken together. Use the following checklist to be sure that you have addressed the large-scale problems that can be missed even after diligent proofing of individual essays:

- Are the main points that I am trying to make evident?

- Do redundancies or apparent contradictions occur between essays?

- Do the essays present a cohesive, coherent image, and does each essay contribute to the same image?

- Is the voice and style used throughout the essays consistent? Does it sound like the same person wrote them?

- Does the essay set support the impression made in the rest of the application?

## CHAPTER 4

# Plan Your Attack

## Chapter Highlights

Using the same essay for more than one school is fine as long as it is tailored to each school and to each question.

Essays about development should focus on your improvement and provide examples. Focus on the new you—do not dwell on the negatives of the old you.

Goal-oriented questions should invoke honest and realistic answers evidenced by prior experiences and a general plan for achieving the goals.

Essays about influences and role models should focus on the effect a particular force has had on you, not on the force itself.

Remember that many activities and accomplishments are already listed on your application, so focus on only one or two that are meaningful. Do not make lists.

Essays about childhood should incorporate a story that relates to who you are today.

Essays about your favorites should include sincere choices and should include why you've chosen a particular subject as well as its meaning to you.

Issue-based essays should demonstrate an ability to objectively consider both sides of an issue and to articulate your reasons for supporting one over the other.

Essays that target a particular school should convey that you have thoroughly researched the school and should include specifics about the school that interest you.

Now that you have thought about the material you want to use in your essays and the focus you want them to have, take some time to think about the questions you need to answer for the different schools. You should already have a sense of the main points you want to make and the areas on which you would like to focus. Now keep in mind creative ways to position your topic in light of the specific questions. Decide where and how to incorporate your main points into each.

To maximize your efforts, make a list of all of the questions you need to answer and carry it around with you for a week or so. Thoughts are like dreams—they can come to us with powerful imagery and emotion, but the clarity fades quickly. If you do not get them down on paper when inspiration hits, you may find them nearly impossible to remember later when you start to write.

If you keep the questions playing in the back of your mind as you go through your day, you will be surprised at some of the creative ideas that pop into your mind. Still, being more proactive in your brainstorming and idea gathering will help speed the process. To assist, we have compiled a list of common question types and essay topics along with strategy tips for tackling each one. Because so many questions are left open or can be interpreted creatively, you will be able to get ideas for strategies from categories unrelated to your specific questions. The best approach to take here is to read through all the sections and not just from the ones that apply to you.

## A Note About Shortcuts—Use Caution

You have probably already figured out that you can save yourself time and energy by tailoring answers to questions for one school for use in similar questions at different schools. If you are creative, you will be able to plug in many of your answers into some not-so-similar questions, too.

The possibilities for swapping data are endless. It is fine to lift whole paragraphs or even entire essays and apply them to different questions—as long as you do so seamlessly. Be absolutely sure that you have answered the question asked. Pay special attention to the introductions and conclusions—this is where cutting and pasting is most evident, because it is usually where direct ties to the question are made.

Thorough proofreading is absolutely imperative if you take shortcuts like these. If a school notices that you have obviously swapped essays without even bothering to tailor them to the questions at hand, it reflects poorly on your sincerity. This also indicates to the admissions committee that this is not your first-choice school.

## Essays About Your Growth and Development

These questions try to find out about you by asking how you have grown and developed over the past few years. Some ask this directly. Others are more creative, such as the question that asks you to attach a picture of yourself and describe how you have grown (see the following example).

Making you compare yourself at two different stages of your life is a clever way to get you to open up about who you really are. Although you do want to show that you have matured, remember that "the child is father of the man." Do not overplay what a terrible person you once were just to make the point of what a great person you are now. No one changes that much in five years. Besides, if the portrait of your former self is more memorable to the admissions team, it should still convey the notion that you were a diamond in the rough.

Remember the essay from the last chapter written by the football player? He spends most of the essay showing us about what an insecure and fearful person he was but then mentions only briefly in the final paragraph that he is now confident and successful. Learn from this example and show, do not tell, how you have changed and who you are now.

Lastly, describe real events and scenarios to prove that your growth resulted from the decisions you made and actions you took. Significant events and people can serve as inspiration. Real change, though, always results from the work, effort, and initiative you have put into yourself. Take credit for your hard work!

## ESSAY 23: Stanford, Picture of Self

When I look at this picture of myself, I realize how much I've grown and changed, not only physically, but also mentally as a person in the last couple of years. Less than one month after this photograph was taken, I arrived at the [school's name] in [school's location] without any idea of what to expect. I entered my second year of high school as an innocent thirteen year-old who was about a thousand miles from home and was a new member of not the sophomore, but "lower-middle" class. Around me in this picture are the things which were most important in my life at the time: studying different types of cars and planes, following Michael Jordan's latest move, and seeing the latest blockbuster show like "Phantom of the Opera" or "Jurassic Park". On my t-shirt is the rest of my life—tennis. Midway through my senior year at the special [school's name] school, the focuses in my life have changed dramatically.

If there is one common occurrence which takes place for every single person in the diverse student body at [school's name], it is that we all grow up much faster for having lived there. I do not know whether this speeding up of the maturing process is generally good or bad, but I definitely have benefited.

The classroom has become a whole different realm for me. Before, the teachers and students alike preached the importance of learning, but it was implicitly obvious that the most important concern was grades. At [school's name] teachers genuinely believe that learning is the most importance objective and deeply encourage us to collaborate with each other and make use of all resources that we may find. In fact, in a certain class this year, my teacher assigned us to prepare every day of the week to discuss a certain book; there were only two requirements in this preparation—we had to maximize our sources, gleaning from everything and everyone in the school, but we were not allowed to actually look at the book. As a result, I know more about that book than any other that I have actually read. It is teaching methods such as this which ensure that we will learn more. Indeed, this matter of "thinking" has been one of the most important aspects of my experience. Whether in Physics or English, I'm required to approach every problem and idea independently and creatively rather than just regurgitate the teacher's words. In discussion with fellow students both inside and outside of class, the complex thoughts flowing through everyone's brain is evident.

However, I believe that the most important concepts which I have espoused in being independent of my parents for half of each year, deal with being a cosmopolitan person. The school's faculty and students are conscious about keeping all of the kids' attention from being based on the school. Every single issue of global concern is brought forth by one group or another whether it be a faculty member, publication, ethnic society, or individual student. Along with being aware of issues of importance, after attending [school's name] my personality has evolved. First, my mannerisms have grown: the school stresses giving respect to everyone and everything. Our former headmaster often said, "Character can be measured not by one's interaction with people who are better off than him or herself, but by one's interactions with those who are worse off." The other prime goal of the school's community is to convert every single timid lower-classman into a loud, rambunctious senior. Basically, if you have an opinion about something, it is wrong not to voice that opinion. Of course, being obnoxious is not the idea. The key is to become a master of communication with teachers, fellow students, all of who are a part of the community, and most importantly, those who are outside of the community.

I do not want to make [school's name] sound as if it produces the perfect students, because it doesn't. But the school deserves a lot of credit for its efforts. Often, some part of the mold does remain. As the college experience approaches, I am still the same person, only modified to better maximize my talents. Although I still have some time to play tennis and see movies, perhaps one of the few similarities between this photograph and me now is my smile.

## Comments

This essay is very well written. The essayist makes boarding school his focus, using it to explain and describe how and why he has changed over the years. A lot of students write about what wonderful people they have become, but they fail to do a good job of understanding and explaining the forces that prevailed to make them change. This writer focuses on the strengths of the school itself. He demonstrates the sort of values it tries to instill in its students such as, "Encouraging us to collaborate with each other and make use of all resources that we may find," and "Giving respect to everyone and everything." Because the writer does so, the reader never doubts that the applicant possesses all the qualities that he credits to the school. Using this method has two advantages. First, the positive, upbeat attitude he has toward his institution is rare. Second, Stanford, for one, recognized that this would reflect well on his ability to adapt to and be a positive force at their school.

## Essays About Goals

You can generally approach questions that ask directly about your plans for the future (What are your career goals, and why did you choose that particular career? How do you see yourself ten years from now?) in one of a few ways. You might already have some realistic and specifically defined goals, such as becoming a social worker or a politician. If this is the case, show that you have built your goal around a true passion and based it in reality. Tie it in with what you have already been involved in and accomplished.

Most students, though, do not yet know exactly what they want to do for a career. If the question allows, you may choose to write about some more personal goals instead. Do you want to have traveled to Africa, or climbed Mount Washington, or run the Boston Marathon by then? Perhaps your goal is something smaller, like learning to play the piano or cook a gourmet meal. Also consider choosing an overriding theme like philanthropy, happiness, or success. Then define the theme in your own terms, and discuss the ways in which you hope it will come into fruition. No matter what you choose, show that it is a realistic goal and not just a pipe dream. You can either outline a game plan or prove that you have already taken the first steps toward reaching your goals.

Many of the questions in this category are worded creatively or ask you to use your imagination. This is intended to get you to loosen up and be yourself. If the question takes you off your guard, let it—it means the committee is looking for an unguarded answer. This makes many applicants uncomfortable. They try to present themselves objectively but end up distancing themselves from the subject matter with overly long words and a dry, academic tone. This is a grave mistake since the whole point of this essay is to reveal something about yourself. The essayist in the following example wrote a fun and creative piece about her idea of an ideal life at 50.

Writing this type of essay also gives you a great opportunity to show the admissions committee that you consider their institution to be an integral step toward attaining your goal. Show them that you have done your research and have chosen them for specific and personal reasons.

## ESSAY 24: University of Pennsylvania, Business, Leisure, and Travel
### Write page 217 of your 300-page autobiography.

and that ended the most terrifying experience of my life.

Surprisingly by age 50, my lucrative business lost its thrill, and I felt like it was time to move on and experience more of what life had to offer. I had enough of the problems and headaches of mainstream life and decided to sell my business to my husband. With a couple million dollars as pocket-money and a picture of my family, I moved to Jamaica where stress is low and "hakuna matata" is the national motto. I wanted to start my new life fresh. I found a perfect, cozy beach house that overlooked the white sand beach and the clear blue ocean. It served as a beautiful sight to collect my thoughts as the waves methodically crashed to shore. While I was overlooking the sea and watching the red-gold sun disappear into the horizon, I realized how truly happy I was. Once again I felt the thrill of new beginnings and the excitement of things to come.

My husband, on the other had, was still heavily involved in the business and insisted on building a pool house with a basement that served as his office. This mock office, fully-equipped with the latest communication technology, enabled him to spend more time with his family, which was our agreement and our compromise. A night-owl and workaholic, my husband frequently worked from dusk until dawn.

My two children, now 20 and 18, are in college having the time of their lives. My son decided to transfer to Oxford while my daughter decided to attend my alma mater. With my children away at school, my husband and I planned a year's vacation around the world. Although he insisted on bringing his mini-fax machine, his pocket computer, and his video-phone on the trip, he promised business would not get in the way, and he kept his promise.

Our first stop—New York. I wanted to marvel in the Statue of Liberty's third renovation and catch the revival of the works of Andrew Lloyd Webber on Broadway. We spent seven glorious days in the Big Apple and reveled in all the urban experiences that we could cram in.

Next stop was Argentina, where we stayed with a family friend in Buenos Aries. The great abundance of food and its high quality leather are two things that stand out in my mind when I look back on our trip. We ate so much food I thought we would be accused of the sin of gluttony, but our only excuse was the fact that our friend served three appetizers, two salads, four main courses, and two desserts with every meal. As for

Argentine leather, I must say its the finest crafted leather we had ever seen. My husband bought so much leather in the form of cowboy boots, pants, and jackets, he look like an over-aged vaquero ready to work on a ranch. As for me, I was glad I got the opportunity to practice my rusty Spanish while bargaining with the leather store owner. We enjoyed Argentina so much that we extended our stay to see the rest of the country, but after a couple weeks of touring, we had to say goodbye to our friend and catch a plane to our next destination, Madagascar with a stop over in Tanzania, Africa.

On our way to Madagascar, we encountered a major problem in

## Comments

This writer took an unusual approach when answering this question by writing about her future. Most students see this question as asking about an incident in their past. This applicant, though, approached it creatively by writing a fun, light-hearted piece about her wildest hopes and dreams. The image of her living it up in the sun at her private pool or traveling the world while her husband slaves away in the basement office or drags along his fax and laptop (to run the business that she sold him) is quite funny and definitely reflects on her spark and wit.

## Essays About Role Models and Influence

This type of question attempts to learn more about you through the forces that have shaped you. Many students make the mistake of believing that this is an essay about a person, trip, or pastime. They go on at length, describing the influence in detail without making a connection between it and themselves. The school is not interested in learning more about a dear relative, a memorable holiday, or a motivational book. They are interested in learning more about you. What aspect(s), specifically, of the book, person, or event made an impression on you, and how? What action did you take to turn this impression into personal development and change?

Colleges learn a lot about your values and standards through your description of your mentors. It is like getting to know a person by the people he chooses to hang out with. If you are skeptical, consider the different impression you would have of the candidate who admires a dynamic, colorful athlete compared with someone who looks up to an accomplished but soft-spoken academic. Neither is better or worse—just different.

There are no wrong answers here. Far more important than who you choose, though, is how you portray that person. In other words, do not choose someone because you think it will impress the committee. Name dropping is not only obvious, it is ineffective. Heed this one word of caution, though. Applicants very commonly pick one of their parents. This does not mean that it is wrong, but it does mean that you will have to do some extra work to make your essay stand out from the crowd.

Some questions about role models aim for the less serious. "If you could walk in someone else's shoes for a day," or "If you could have lunch with any person dead or alive." Whereas the other role model questions ask for mentors, this question asks for heroes. You do not need to be as realistic in your response—feel free to loosen up and have fun. However, always consider what the committee members will infer from your choice. Why did you choose that person? Was it because he or she is similar or dissimilar to you? Did you choose to write about that individual because of what you could learn or to effect a change?

## ESSAY 25: Wellesley, Influence of Mother

It took me eighteen years to realize what an extraordinary influence my mother has been on my life. She's the kind of person who has thoughtful discussions about which artist she would most want to have her portrait painted by (Sargent), the kind of mother who always has time for her four children, and the kind of community leader who has a seat on the board of every major project to assist Washington's impoverished citizens. Growing up with such a strong role model, I developed many of her enthusiasms. I not only came to love the excitement of learning simply for the sake of knowing something new, but I also came to understand the idea of giving back to the community in exchange for a new sense of life, love, and spirit.

My mother's enthusiasm for learning is most apparent in travel. I was nine years old when my family visited Greece. Every night for three weeks before the trip, my older brother Peter and I sat with my mother on her bed reading Greek myths and taking notes on the Greek Gods. Despite the fact that we were traveling with fourteen-month-old twins, we managed to be at each ruin when the site opened at sunrise. I vividly remember standing in an empty ampitheatre pretending to be an ancient tragedian, picking out my favorite sculpture in the Acropolis museum, and inserting our family into modified tales of the battle at Troy. Eight years and half a dozen passport stamps later I have come to value what I have learned on these journeys about global history, politics and culture, as well as my family and myself.

While I treasure the various worlds my mother has opened to me abroad, my life has been equally transformed by what she has shown me just two miles from my house. As a ten year old, I often accompanied my mother to [name deleted], a local soup kitchen and children's center. While she attended meetings, I helped with the Summer Program by chasing children around the building and performing magic tricks. Having finally perfected the "floating paintbrush" trick, I began work as a full time volunteer with the five and six year old children last June. It is here that I met Jane Doe, an exceptionally strong girl with a vigor that is contagious. At the end of the summer, I decided to continue my work at [name deleted] as Jane's tutor. Although the position is often difficult, the personal rewards are beyond articulation. In the seven years since I first walked through the doors of [name deleted], I have learned not only the idea of giving to others, but also of deriving from them a sense of spirit.

Everything that my mother has ever done has been overshadowed by the thought behind it. While the raw experiences I have had at home and abroad have been spectacular, I have learned to truly value them by watching my mother. She has enriched my life with her passion for learning, and changed it with her devotion to humanity. In her endless love of everything and everyone she is touched by, I have seen a hope and life that is truly exceptional. Next year, I will find a new home miles away. However, my mother will always be by my side.

## Comments

The topic of this essay is the writer's mother. However, the writer definitely focuses on herself, which makes this essay so strong. She manages to impress the reader with her travel experience, volunteer and community experience, and commitment to learning without ever sounding boastful. The essay is also very well organized.

## Essays About Achievements

Your answer to questions like "Describe a significant challenge you have faced," and "Describe your greatest accomplishment" say a lot more about you than simply what you have accomplished. It will show the committee what you value, what makes you proud, and what you are capable of accomplishing. A common mistake made in answering this question is repeating information that can be found elsewhere in the application. A good student, for example, will be tempted to fall back on stressing his or her high G.P.A. or S.A.T. score. A person who has won a number of awards or acknowledgments will try to include all of them and end up turning his or her essay into little more than a prose list.

If you do choose to write about an accomplishment that the committee can read about somewhere else on your application, be sure to bring the experience alive by demonstrating what it took to get there and how it affected you personally. Do not be afraid to show them that you feel proud. This is not the place for modesty. However, do not fall to the other extreme either—you can toot your own horn, but do it without being didactic or preachy. You will not have to worry about either extreme if you spend the bulk of your essay simply telling the story.

If you feel like you have not done anything worth focusing on, then remind yourself that the best essays are often about modest accomplishments. It does not matter what you accomplished as long as it was personally meaningful and you can make it come alive. Unless specified, the accomplishment can be professional, personal, or academic. Did you get a compliment from a notoriously tight-lipped, hard-driving boss during a summer job? Did you lose the race but beat your own best time? Did you work around the clock to bring your C in physics up to an A? Do not think about what they want to hear—think about what has really made you proud.

## ESSAY 26: Michigan, Time-management Skill

One of my most important talents has to be my ability to manage time wisely. My passion for involvement in school activities has far surpassed any simple desire, it has become a minor neurosis. All these activities could crowd out my schoolwork, but luckily enough, I've been able to balance my schedule rather nicely. But what if they somehow happened to coincide, to somehow fall in one day? Be prepared for A NOT SO TYPICAL, BUT VERY POSSIBLE, DAY IN THE LIFE OF [name].

It's 6:45 a.m. and I'm in the shower. Normally I would wake up earlier to take care of that task, but I didn't need to wake up in the morning. Five days and several drafts after starting my King Lear paper I still couldn't tie the theme of justice to filial ingratitude. Solution: pull an all-nighter. In my characteristic euphemistic manner, I like to refer to the whole fiasco as my way of easing myself into the wonderful world of term papers. By 7:30 I'm in my first-hour class, ironically, but expectedly, bright-eyed, although not as bushy-tailed as normal. After school, I prepare for the rough time I'm about to have juggling all of my extracurriculars. I also realize that I won't be returning home for a prolonged period of time. Boy, do I miss that lunch hour this year. It's really hard to convince myself that taking extra elective classes are worth corporal punishment, but thinking of the supply-demand curves I learned in Economics, all doubt leaves my mind. Nonetheless, I scurry to the Writing Center for my hour of tutoring. After completing my thesis-teaching, participle-undangling duties, I rush off to my National Honor Society Meeting where I preside over the board and arrange plans for this year's Special Olympics. I find both of those activities very rewarding because of the service that accompanies them. Not only do I share my talents and abilities with the less fortunate, but I also learn as much as the people I help because I view my own abilities from a different perspective. I learn to appreciate my talents like that lost lunch hour and learn how to put them to even greater use by sharing them. By 4 p.m., I also appreciate that the Student Advisory Committee meets during school. While that forces me to miss class, in turn giving me even more homework, I would rather not have to rush talking with the principal about matters concerning administrative policy and how it affects students. As far as I'm concerned, if school decisions don't get student input they're meaningless. Nor will I hesitate to put that in writing in the school newspaper. So at four o'clock I head into the computer lab an hour late in order to publish the next issue of the [school newspaper]. My staff adviser is somewhat mad at me because of the angered reaction the School Board had toward my biting editorial on administrative waste (true story), so in a somewhat self-confident way I mention that my national award wasn't won by waffling on tough stories. This issue seems to be going well as far as layout, and it looks like I might get to go home as early as eight o'clock. So I thought. In that funny way Fate has of reminding us not to guess the future, the Entertainment Editor mis-sizes an ad, forcing the whole page to have to be redone. Moments like those make me want to quit the paper, but I enjoy the writing and planning of the periodical too much to ever make my threats serious. I also feel it is my duty to inform the school about events that concern students, especially unfair ones, and to state my opinion on such policies. Without that service, many would be in the dark about very important issues. I view that as a tragedy.

I finally leave at 9:30, and return home to eat, study for tomorrow's JETS competition, plan out debate arguments, do homework, and make up for yesterday night's lost sleep—all within a four hour period. So much for finishing that T.S. Eliot anthology I enjoy. It's always difficult to put aside something one likes to do, and I still don't understand how I sacrificed my love for science for other activities. Ever since I perused my first science book in the first grade, I've had a love for the subject which only intensified when I began getting hands-on experience, engineering experience, from projects I copied out of library books. I miss electrolysis, making devices from mousetraps and my first-place science fair project. Studying engineering would allow me to put my interest and abilities in that field to use for others as I enjoy doing with every activity. If only I had a University of Michigan engineering degree to help me design a solution to that problem.

## Comments

This essay's strength lies in how detailed and specific the author gets by walking the reader through a day in his life. He writes with a light tone that somewhat helps to modify some of his more boastful claims. He manages to talk about a very wide range of interests by tying it all in to the focus of his schedule for that day. This essay could have been improved, though, by not trying as hard to impress by mentioning King Lear, the National Honors Society, the JETS competition, and his position on the newspaper. When taken all together, this is apt to sound too much like name dropping. He would have done better by leaving some of these out (they are, after all, listed elsewhere in his application) and concentrating on showing more depth in just one or two of the areas.

## Essays About Hobbies and Interests

Questions about your extracurricular activities and interests ("Describe a significant interest or value," "What do you do for fun?" "Write about a meaningful activity") are important for showing the committee that you are a well-rounded and passionate person. Show that you are dedicated, funny, offbeat, or interesting—after all, these types of traits make people and essays more exciting. Communicate feelings of passion, commitment, and devotion. Wherever possible, also demonstrate the leadership abilities you have developed in these activities.

As with all questions, you cannot write any wrong answers here. Do not feel that you need to limit yourself to the standard type of school-related extracurriculars like playing sports or helping with the literary magazine. This book contains essays describing a wide variety of interests. Essayist 47, for example, writes about her pen-pal relationships. Essayist 33 writes passionately about his interest in philosophy. The writers of both Essay 10 and Essay 13 write about debating. Essay 8 focuses on the visual arts.

## Essays About Childhood Experiences

Some questions directly ask for stories from your youth, such as "Please define your current personality with anecdotes from your childhood." These essays can be particularly fun to write. To answer many other questions as well, you can highlight a point with a childhood anecdote or focus on how your upbringing has affected who you are now. This is a great opportunity to tell a story using as many colorful details as possible. You must, however, remember to relate the anecdote to who you are today.

## ESSAY 27: Cornell, Childhood Anecdotes

**Please define your current personality with anecdotes from your childhood.**

By unlocking the door to [name] past, one sees his thoughts and actions when they first took hold of his persona. This essay serves as a key to that door and to my current personality.

The first beloved books in my life were the Sesame Street Encyclopedia volumes. At three, I wasn't old enough to read them, but I always wanted to have them read to me. In fact, I memorized the ten volume set so when my parents would skip some pages I would ask them to read what they skipped. After learning to read on my own, my favorite book became the anatomy volume in the Charlie Brown Encyclopedia. Courtesy of a supermarket book offer, I was the only kindergartner who knew about fertilized egg cells. As I grew older, I continued to read largely because reading taught me so much outside of what we learned in school.

Since kindergarten, my extensive reading also originated my various interests, especially in science. Living within walking distance of the library, I went there every day, enabling me to dabble in a different subject during each visit. By the fourth grade, I had read all the chemistry books containing fewer than 200 pages, by the fifth grade I was reading about Einstein's Theory of Relativity. During that time period, I became so interested in astronomy through Odyssey Magazine that I sold holiday cards door-to-door in order to buy a telescope.

Reading also helped me in school. A little ingenuity didn't hurt, either. For example, as part of my third grade reading grade, I needed to do some independent reading. Every sixty pages in a book counted for one star of credit and in order to get an "A," I needed fifteen stars. I was greedy and saw this as an opportunity to shine far above the rest of my classmates. Instead of reading many short books, I devoured 300-page sagas by Laura Ingalls Wilder. When everyone else got eighteen stars, the little banana with my name on it had 45. This inner drive and competition still motivates my work today, but unfortunately, no one gives out stars anymore.

Despite this desire to do my best, I was quite normal, except for a slight perfectionist's twist to everything. I too owned a cabbage patch doll, but it was taken away because I cared for it excessively. On one Halloween, I dressed up as Dracula just like a dozen other kids, but I wanted my hair to look so realistic that it took a week to wash out all the gel I used. Finally, much like any other child, I fantasized about adventures, but I took fantasizing one step further. I recorded my make-believe adventures on tape so they could be critiqued afterward.

One of the few things I was not a perfectionist at was my writing. Due to a lack of self-confidence, I would plan papers well in advance but put them off until the very last minute. This habit continues today, accounting for the transition-lacking stream-of-consciousness style found in almost all my writing. I just hope it appeals to Cornell admissions officers.

## Comments

This writer undoubtedly made an impression as a child with his voracious reading skills. He is unfortunately a little too aware of this throughout the essay. His attempt to make himself appear driven and ambitious ends up coming across as a bit over the top, and one wonders how such an extreme perfectionist will be able to take the pressures of college life. He could have also done without the bashing of his writing skills in the last paragraph. This display of insecurity undercuts the overconfident tone of the rest of the piece, making the reader suspect that it might have been more bravado and a desire to impress than his true voice.

## Essays About Your Favorite . . .

Writing about an influential book, character, or historical figure intimidates even the best students. The best strategy is to stop worrying about what the committee will think of your choice and simply be honest. If you cannot decide between favorites, try selecting a quality that you consider representative of yourself as a whole. Then select a book, a person, an issue, or an incident that sheds light on this quality.

If at all possible, avoid obvious choices designed to impress an admissions committee, like Abraham Lincoln, Mother Teresa, or *The Canterbury Tales*, unless they have a real, personal meaning to you. Even then, reconsider. Pick somebody you have a genuine admiration for, whether famous or obscure. Support it with observations, reactions, opinions, perceptions, and reflections. Subjective support is better than objective facts because, once again, it reveals something about you.

## ESSAY 28: Harvard, Favorite Characters

Of all the characters that I've "met" through books and movies, two stand out as people that I most want to emulate. They are Atticus Finch from *To Kill A Mockingbird* and Dr. Archibald "Moonlight" Graham from *Field of Dreams*. They appeal to me because they embody what I strive to be. They are influential people in small towns who have a direct positive effect on those around them. I, too, plan to live in a small town after graduating from college, and that positive effect is something I must give in order to be satisfied with my life.

Both Mr. Finch and Dr. Graham are strong supporting characters in wonderful stories. They symbolize good, honesty, and wisdom. When the story of my town is written I want to symbolize those things. The base has been formed for me to live a productive, helpful life. As an Eagle Scout I represent those things that Mr. Finch and Dr. Graham represent. In the child/adolescent world I am Mr. Finch and Dr. Graham, but soon I'll be entering the adult world, a world in which I'm not yet prepared to lead.

I'm quite sure that as teenagers Atticus Finch and Moonlight Graham often wondered what they could do to help others. They probably emulated someone who they had seen live a successful life. They saw someone like my grandfather, 40-year president of our hometown bank, enjoy a lifetime of leading, sharing, and giving. I have seen him spend his Christmas Eves taking gifts of food and joy to indigent families. Often when his bank could not justify a loan to someone in need, my grandfather made the loan from his own pocket. He is a real-life Moonlight Graham, a man who has shown me that characters like Dr. Graham and Mr. Finch do much much more than elicit tears and smiles from readers and movie watchers. Through him and others in my family I feel I have acquired the values and the burning desire to benefit others that will form the foundation for a great life. I also feel that that foundation is not enough. I do not yet have the sophistication, knowledge, and wisdom necessary to succeed as I want to in the adult world. I feel that Harvard, above all others, can guide me toward the life of greatness that will make me the Atticus Finch of my town.

## Comments

This essay is a great example of how to answer this question well. This applicant chose characters who demonstrated specific traits that reflect on his own personality. We believe that he is sincere about his choices because his reasons are personal (being from a small town, and so forth). He managed to tell us a good deal about himself, his values, and his goals while maintaining a strong focus throughout.

## Essays About Social Issues and Current Affairs

Questions that ask your opinions about social or political movements or current affairs are among the hardest to answer. Even here you need to stay personal.

However, discussing an issue of broad social concern can be difficult. If a cause is important to you or you have a strong opinion about it, relate it back to your life. What about you, your experiences, or your upbringing has made this issue resonate for you? Why do you care? Does the issue affect you personally in any way?

Be sure to write about both sides of the issue to show that you can think objectively and logically. Showing that you are passionate is great; showing that you are one sided or bull headed is not. One applicant who answered this question well is the writer of Essay 36, who chose the Middle East peace debate as his focus. He names why the issue is close to him (because he is a Jewish-American who debates the issue at his private Jewish school). The writer presents both sides with a level head, briefly explaining why he is on the side of the opposition.

Refrain from making sweeping generalizations or commenting about issues that would be out of your range of experience. Essayist 48 falls into this trap when he writes about medical ethics. One admissions officer found his assertion that there have been no ethical considerations in the medical field until recently to be "simply wrong." "Whoa, boy. Easy, Trigger! This writer dives in way over his/her head" reacts another. To avoid this response, the writer could have focused more on the experience of his brother's illness and why it made this issue personal for him. As with all your essays, getting good feedback will be key.

## Essays That Target the School

Knowing the schools to which you apply is an essential step in answering any essay, but some questions ask you to write about them directly. When answering a question such as "Why do you want to go to [school's name]," show that you understand what the school has to offer in your anticipated area of study or extracurricular involvement. Mention specific factors that tie in with your area of interest. Doing this will help you to avoid the insincere, ingratiating tone that is a danger in this type of essay. Each point will be honest and well supported, thereby lending credibility to the essay and, in turn, to you.

Another challenge is finding a balanced yet truthful tone. Do not be cocky or self-effacing. Show a solid, well-researched knowledge of the school. Be honest and be thorough. If you cannot find any connections, you might want to return to Chapter 2 to gather more material about your schools.

### ESSAY 29: Georgetown, School Target

When I think of Georgetown University, I think of Washington and world affairs. I do not know yet exactly what type of professional career I will pursue after schooling, but I do know that I wish to be internationally aware and involved, and that Georgetown would provide me with a solid foundation for that goal.

I am glad I do not know specifically what I want to do later on, because it should be an adventure choosing which course I will take in life. Thus, I have time to experiment and learn from a wide variety of topics. At Georgetown, I am presented with the opportunity to take any classes I want and to be taught by some of the most learned and dynamic professors in the world. I was once told that in college, I "will take classes in subjects I had never thought or heard of," and I am very excited to do this.

If I were required to pick a major at this instant, I would choose history. If history were only studying, memorizing and regurgitating events, facts, and dates, I would be just as uninterested as most people. However, in studying history, I get a chance to contemplate ideologies and the nature of human beings. I believe that Georgetown University is the best place in the world to study history. It is a school located in Washington, D.C., the capital of the country, of outstanding academic reputation and recognition; my resources would be absolutely unlimited. Living in Washington, I would feel the pulse of our world today. The United States is the world's dominant power and every issue of great global importance is brought to the country's capital.

I have been told that although Georgetown has approximately 6,000 undergraduates, the students and faculty alike feel as if the school is a small, interwoven community. I believe that this sense of closeness is a vital aspect in an outstanding college experience. We learn most from interactions among other people, and the fact that this reputation of faculty accessibility and student involvement—both in the immediate Georgetown community and in Washington, D.C.—exists, is very attractive to me.

## ESSAY 30: Johns Hopkins, School Target

The college admissions and selection process is a very important one, perhaps one that will have the greatest impact on one's future. The college that a person will go to often influences his personality, views, and career. Therefore, when I hear people say that "it doesn't matter that much which college you go to. You can get a good education anywhere, if you are self-motivated," I tend to be rather skeptical. Perhaps, as far as actual knowledge is concerned, that statement is somewhat valid. Physics and mathematics are the same, regardless of where they are taught. Knowledge, however, is only a small piece of the puzzle that is college, and it is in the rest of that puzzle that colleges differ.

At least as important, or even more important, than knowledge, is the attitude towards that knowledge. Last year, when my engineering team was competing in the NEDC Design Challenge, held at Hopkins, after the competition I and a few friends talked to a professor of civil engineering. What struck me is the passion with which he talked about his field of study. At Hopkins, everyone—the students, the faculty, the administration—displays a certain earnestness about learning. This makes Hopkins a good match for me, as I, too, am very enthusiastic about the subjects I study. I love learning, and when those around me do too, it creates a great atmosphere from which everyone benefits.

My enthusiasm and activeness extend not just to academics, but to other aspects of life as well. I am very involved in extracurricular activities, participating in my school's engineering club and math team, and I love sports, having played on the varsity soccer and tennis teams for three years. This makes Hopkins, with its great sport traditions and a multitude of clubs and organizations, a great choice. Further, while in college I intend to explore new activities. Because of my school's small size and dual curriculum, there is a relatively narrow spectrum of activities available for me. Hopkins affords a great opportunity for me to branch out and participate in organizations to which I previously had no access.

Another aspect of Hopkins that attracts me greatly is its student body, diverse and multicultural, but at the same time uniformly strong academically. Since I myself am a refugee from Russia, where I experienced social and cultural anti-semitism, multiculturalism and acceptance of different groups are very important to me, not to mention that it allows me to meet people of different backgrounds and learn of their varying perspectives. And this summer at the U.S.A. Mathematical Talent Search Young Scholars' Program, I experienced the thrill of working in a group where everyone is on the same, or higher, intellectual level as I. I think that, given my academic and cultural background, I would fit in well with the student life at Hopkins and contribute to it.

Academically, too, I believe I would fit Hopkins well. Though Hopkins is most known for its medical program, its engineering school is also one of the best, and that is the general area of study I intend to pursue. In high school, I've most enjoyed my mathematics and science courses, particularly physics, and I have participated in the engineering school, so attending Hopkins' engineering program would be a natural extension of my high school interests. However, my interests are not confined solely to the sciences. I enjoy courses from all areas of curriculum, particularly unorthodox and thought-provoking ones. Therefore, Hopkins, which according to the viewbook "is geared toward educating students in the fundamentals of their field of interest while illuminating wider possibilities through interdisciplinary study" is perfect for me.

Of course, none of those aspects of Hopkins, neither their great student body, their world-renowned faculty, their research centers, nor their clubs and extracurricular opportunities, are worth anything unless one takes advantage of them. That, however, is exactly what I intend to do. While many people find the transition to college overwhelming, therefore not participating in the student life fully the first year, I hope to plunge immediately into the full array of possibility and make as much use of them as possible. Though my soccer and tennis skills might prove insufficient to earn me a place on Hopkins' varsity teams (though I hope that's not the case,) I nevertheless want to play sports at least on the club level. Other than that, however, nothing is set in stone except for one thing—to take as full and broad advantage of what Hopkins has to offer as possible.

## Comments

Both of these essays do a good job of showing that the writers know the schools and have some specific reasons for wanting to attend them. The first focuses more on the academic environment and surrounding city. The second combines several aspects such as academics, extracurriculars, and a diverse student body. Both applicants also use the opportunity to show that they would fit in by highlighting their own interests and activities (an interest in history in the first and math, tennis, and soccer in the second).

## Essays About International Experience

If you have had some interesting travel experiences or an unusual international background, you may want to use this as the focus in one of your essays. You will be able to highlight this experience or background in answer to almost any question. Doing so can go a long way in differentiating yourself from the crowd. Show both how and why the experience has affected you. Make the experience itself interesting. Use vivid and colorful details, as the writer of Essay 37 did. Explain how the experience or background has changed you and what you have taken away from it, as Essayist 32 did.

## Essays About Family

Writing about your family life and background can be natural and easy for some applicants but daunting for others. Few questions ask about your family life directly, so for most writers it is a choice. For those who do not have the choice, remember that no family is ideal. You need not have had 1.5 siblings, a dog, and a white picket fence in order to write comfortably about your family. In fact, a unique background will set you apart. Still, this is no place to air dirty laundry. If a question about your family has you staring uncomfortably at a blank page, then stop thinking about trying to describe your entire family history in a few paragraphs. Just think of two or three defining qualities or characteristics of your home life, and use one or two specific incidents to illustrate them. After you have done so, you will find that by focusing on the parts, you have painted an accurate picture of the whole.

One pitfall that you want to avoid is seeming so attached to your family that the transition away from them into college will be difficult. One example of a student who made this mistake is Essayist 55. "I have always been a bit leery," writes one officer in response, "of essays that stress so much the loyalty to one's family. College is a time for loosening ties to family somewhat, and learning to think and act independently. Please understand that I am not, by any means, criticizing love and loyalty to one's family. But an admission officer will want to feel sure that the applicant will be able to establish a vibrant life in an environment far removed from the immediate family." Note, though, that the bad marks this essay received resulted more from the lack of detail and color rather than from the subject.

Congratulations! You have made it through all the preparatory steps needed to write the best essay possible. Give yourself a pat on the back; you are almost done. "But how can that be possible," you may ask, "when I have not even started writing yet?"

If you followed all the steps prior to this one, then you should have a clear picture in your mind of what you plan to say and how you plan to say it. All you have to do now is transfer the essay from your mind to the paper. Believe it or not, this step is easier than you think.

Writing is difficult only when you do not know what points you want to make, have not decided which material to use to make your points, or are insecure about your writing skills. If you have been following along through the information and exercises of the first four chapters, then you have addressed the first two potential problems already. The next chapter is designed to help you get past the third. It takes you step-by-step through the process of actually writing an essay, using plenty of examples along the way. So put your anxieties aside and get ready to write.

# CHAPTER 5

# At Last, Write!

---

## Chapter Highlights

Creating an outline will help you write structured and effective essays.

Paragraphs should contain a clear beginning, middle, and end.

Each paragraph should contain one central thought.

The first sentence of each paragraph should provide a smooth transition from the last.

Overuse of a thesaurus is transparent.

Use verbs over adverbs and adjectives as much as possible.

Avoid sentences that are excessively long, or frequent use of sentences that are too short.

An effective lead should capture your reader's attention and be relevant to the essay.

Introductions should not be forced—beginning with a story can be the best approach.

Conclusions should be memorable, but they should not be a summary of the essay.

Essay titles are not necessary.

---

Now that you know what you want to say in each of your essays, it is time to start writing. First, set a time limit of no more than one day for each essay. The longer your time frame, the more difficult it will be to write your first draft. The point is this: do not allow yourself to sit around waiting for inspiration to strike. As one admissions officer said, "Some of the worst writing ever crafted has been done under the guise of inspiration."

Relieve some of the pressure of writing by reminding yourself that this is just a draft. Rid yourself of the notion that your essay can be perfect on the first try. Do not agonize over a particular word choice or the phrasing of an idea—you will have plenty of time to perfect the essay later. For now, you just need to start. The most important thing is to get the words onto paper or a computer screen.

## Creating an Outline

The easiest way to sabotage all the work you have done so far is to skip this step. Writing is as much a discipline as it is an art. To ensure that your essays flow well and make sense, you need to construct solid outlines before you write. Unless you conscientiously impose structure around your ideas, your essays will be rambling and ineffective without an outline.

Based on the information you have developed throughout the last chapters, choose one essay, and construct an outline that contains the central idea as well as its supporting points. At its most basic, an outline will be as simple as this:

*Paragraph 1*
   Introduction that contains the central idea

*Paragraph 2*
   Topic sentence that ties into the central idea
   First supporting point
   Evidence for point

*Paragraph 3*
   Topic sentence that links the above paragraph to the next
   Second supporting point
   Evidence for point

*Paragraph 4*
   Topic sentence that links the above paragraph to the next
   Third supporting point
   Evidence for point

*Paragraph 5*
   Conclusion that reiterates the central idea and takes it one step further

An outline should make sense on its own. The ideas should follow logically in the order that you list them. Adding content around these main points should support and reinforce the logic of the outline. Finally, the outline should conclude with an insightful thought or image. Make sure that the rest of your outline reinforces this conclusion.

You can take this simple outline structure and apply it to the material you have in many different ways. Look, for example, at Essay 25 written in response to a question about influence.

*Paragraph 1 (Introduction)*
   *Leading sentence:* "It took me eighteen years to realize what an extraordinary influence my mother has been on my life."

*Summary of main points:* "I not only came to love the excitement of learning simply for the sake of knowing something new, but I also came to understand the idea of giving back to the community in exchange for a new sense of life, love, and spirit."

*Paragraph 2 (First Supporting Point)*

*Transition sentence:* "My mother's enthusiasm for learning is most apparent in travel."

*Supporting point:* Her mother's enthusiasm for learning.

*Evidence:* Learning through travel by using the example of a trip to Greece.

*Paragraph 3 (Second Supporting Point)*

*Transition sentence:* "While I treasure the various worlds my mother has opened to me abroad, my life has been equally transformed by what she has shown me just two miles from my house."

*Supporting point:* Her mother's dedication to the community.

*Evidence:* Her multiple volunteer activities such as helping at the local soup kitchen.

*Paragraph 4 (Conclusion)*

*Transition sentence:* "Everything that my mother has ever done has been overshadowed by the thought behind it."

*Reiteration of main points:* "She has enriched my life with her passion for learning, and changed it with her devotion to humanity."

*Taking it one step further:* "Next year, I will find a new home miles away. However, my mother will always be by my side."

Although almost all good outlines will follow this general structure, you can modify it in multiple ways according to the type of essay you want to write.

## Structured Does Not Mean Stiff

You might be thinking: "But I am writing a creative essay; I don't need to have structure!"

Wrong. All essays need structure—even creative ones. Being creative or unusual does not give you license to be sloppy or careless—not if you expect to make a good impression. If you are going to take a creative approach, do it with the same kind of planning and organization that you would put into any other important piece of writing.

On a similar note, you do not need to be dry, boring, or academic to appear logical and well ordered. What makes an essay interesting and inventive is its topic, word choice, and imagery—not its lack of organization. Remember, the most creative and colorful writing in the world—poetry—is also the most structured, planned, and precise.

Like a poem, your essay does not need to follow the traditional outline presented above to be well structured. There are as many different ways to structure a piece of writing as there are pieces of writing. To gather ideas for the best way to structure yours, read through the descriptions and examples of some of the basics provided below.

## The Example Structure

This is a good structure to use when you want to make a single, strong point. Its power lies in its simplicity. Because it allows you to present several points neatly in support of a single claim, it is especially useful when you are trying to be persuasive or make an argument. However, you can certainly use it in response to almost any kind of question.

For an example of this type of structure, look at Essay 36. The writer takes the first two paragraphs to introduce his argument. (He probably could have done without the first. For more about this, see the section "Beginnings and Endings.") He states his position in the last sentence of the second paragraph, "I adhere to the views of the Likud (opposition) party, which opposes the peace process." The next paragraph addresses the first example of arguments against his position, "The accusation . . . of promoting war and violence." The next addresses the second, "The question of whether they have the right to influence Israeli policy." The fifth paragraph addresses the third example, being "identified with condoning the assassination [of Yitzhak Rabin]." The last paragraph summarizes and restates his argument and then takes it one step further by concluding that the debate has "demonstrated the necessity of objectiveness and removal of emotions from the discussion."

## Chronological Structure

To facilitate smooth transitions, you might apply a chronological approach to your outline. The sequence of events will help reinforce flow from one stage of the essay to the next. One downfall of this approach is that you may create an essay that reads like a ship's log. Be sure that the element of time does not stifle the message you want to convey through the story. Do not feel obligated to tell more of the story than you need to convey your point adequately.

The chronological method does not have to span many years or even months. Essay 26 used it to demonstrate the events of a single day. It begins with an introduction stating his main point, time-management skills. The second paragraph begins at the start of his day, 6:45 A.M. It proceeds through to 7:30 A.M. when he is in his first class, then 4:00 P.M. when he is heading into the computer lab. He begins the last paragraph at 9:30 P.M. and concludes by restating his argument. He takes it one step further by addressing that he wishes he could do even more in one day. He finishes in the last sentence with a catchy and clever statement, "If only I had a University of Michigan engineering degree to help me design a solution to that problem."

## Description Structure

This is similar to the chronological structure except that instead of walking step-by-step through increments of time, it follows step-by-step through a description of a place, person, or thing. An example of this would be Essay 46, which takes the reader through a tour of his bedroom. The first paragraph gives an introduction describing the general feel of the room. The second describes "the room's workspace, my desk and computer." The third turns to the "relaxation area, commonly referred to as a bed." The last paragraph completes the tour by stepping out (literally) with, "After exiting my room, I would hope my visitor learned a few important things about me," and offering a brief conclusion of what the room says about him.

## Compare and Contrast

Some questions make using this structure a natural choice, such as the personal growth and development question, which asks you to compare yourself now to the way you once were. Essay 28 uses this structure by comparing the author's two favorite book characters to the person he would like to become and to the person his grandfather was. Essay 4 is another example of this type of structure. It introduces a comparison in the third paragraph, "With one hand on the tiller and the other holding the mainsheet, I see that my hands are in the same position when I play my bass guitar. Comparisons between the two mesh together in my mind as I realize the similarities between bass guitar and sailing." After comparing the two activities point for point, he sums up with, "Bass guitar and sailing do not seem to relate to one another, but I discover the similarities."

Like this example, you can structure a cause-and-effect essay point for point by comparing one aspect of the object or situation at a time. You can also choose to employ the block method. Thoroughly cover all the points of the first object or situation in the first half of the essay and then compare it with all the points of the other in the last half.

## Cause and Effect

Cause-and-effect essays usually depict a before-and-after experience and are often used in response to questions about influence. Using this structure can highlight that you understand and appreciate the effect that other people and situations have on your growth, development, and maturity.

The writer of Essay 2, for example, wrote about the effect that playing football had on him. Before football, he writes, he was "shy, had low self-esteem and turned away from seemingly impossible challenges." However, his success at the game and the "months of tough practices" taught him "what it takes to succeed" and gave him a work ethic and self-confidence.

If you decide to use this structure, be sure you do not write yourself out of the equation. Try to make the point that you were the catalyst between the cause and the effect. That way you demonstrate that you know how to take action and create change.

## Narrative

Structuring your essay as a narrative (by telling a story) is a common and effective method for keeping the reader's interest. Your essay will take this structure if you have decided to focus on a single event in your life. A narrative essay can itself be structured in many ways. The example of the chronological essay about time management is a type of narrative. However, in its purest form, the narrative essay does nothing but tell the story. It begins and ends with the action.

The following are all examples of pure narrative:

**Essay 38:** It tells the story of a martial arts competition. It begins with the writer's getting some sleep the night before. The essay follows him through breakfast and is with him as he drives to the competition. It climaxes with the actual competition as he "drove a solitary fist to its mark." Very action oriented, it spans one day.

**Essay 39:** This essay is about attending the National High School Orchestra. It starts with the writer boarding the plane for Cincinnati and is with her as she picks up her room key and makes her first friends. It tells about practicing, auditioning, having dinner in the cafeteria, and finding the results of the audition. The essay continues on the second day with rehearsals and climaxes with the playing of the orchestra. "My emotion soared, wafted by the beauty and artfulness of the music, bringing goose-bumps to my skin and a joyful feeling to my soul." This essay spans several days.

**Essay 44:** It tells of a hospital visit to see grandmother. The essay begins with the writer and grandmother smiling at each other. It moves to conversation between mother and grandmother and the writer's thoughts about each. The climax of action is the writer's hand moving to touch the grandmother's forehead, followed by the doctor's announcement that her tests turned out negative. It spans minutes.

Notice the variety of circumstances this type of essay can be applied to when comparing these essays. A narrative can span a lifetime or a moment. It can be filled with action or with subtle looks and movements. It does not have to be filled with Hollywood-style action to hold interest. The briefest and simplest of events can take on meaning when told effectively. What makes all of these essays effective is their use of detail, description, and direction. If you are going to take the narrative approach, learn from these examples. Keep events moving forward. Describe events, people, and places in specific terms; for example, she flew to Cincinnati, he drove for two hours, hands knitted bright tricolored scarves. Finally, do not add reflective conclusions or introductions describing what you learned. Start and end with the action, and have everything take place within the context of the story.

Narrative can be combined with other structures for an approach that is less risky but still interesting. Beginning an essay with a brief story is the most common and effective method of doing this. Essayist 32 does so when she begins with the story of overhearing two Swiss women talking about American culture.

A twist on the narrative essay is one that describes a single place, person, or action in great detail. It appeals to the senses of the audience without necessarily drawing on the action of a story. This type of essay has no standard structure—each is differently organized, but all rely purely on crisp imagery and sensory detail. It does not tell a story or build to a climax. When done well, it leaves the reader with a single, vivid image. Single images are easier to remember than a list of points, qualities, traits, or qualifications no matter how impressive any one or all of them are.

This is a risky approach. It is best employed when you have to provide multiple essays for one school, leaving you with a chance to structure your other essays more traditionally.

## Paragraphs

Paragraphs are the pillars of the essay—they uphold and support the structure. Each one that you write should express a single thought and contain a beginning, a middle, and an end. Again, this holds true whether you are writing a traditional or a creative essay.

Look at Essay 1 for an example of what we mean by writing solid paragraphs. His essay consists of six paragraphs. Notice that each one contains a single thought, phrase, or image introduced by a topic sentence and supported by concrete evidence or imagery.

*Paragraph 1:*

*Introduction.* It begins with, "A creek is no place for shoes." It introduces the essay by describing the creek.

*Paragraph 2:*

*First point.* It begins with, "The creek often taught me things; it was my mentor." It offers supporting evidence of learning about metamorphosis from the tadpoles he collected there.

*Paragraph 3:*

*Second point.* It begins with, "By the creek, my mind was free to wander." He describes himself daydreaming by the side of the creek.

*Paragraph 4:*

*Third point.* It begins with, "I was always up for a challenge." It provides evidence of balance and agility games with his sister.

*Paragraph 5:*

*Fourth point.* It begins with, "The creek was a frontier." He describes pushing the boundaries as he got older by taking expeditions.

*Paragraph 6:*

*Conclusion.* It transitions with, "Years later, I happened to be walking to a friend's house by way of the creek. It occurred to me that what was once an expedition was now merely a shortcut." He summarizes and connects back to all main points with, "Although I had left this place behind, I found others: new questions and freedoms, new challenges and places to explore." It ends with a closing sentence, "But this creek would remain foremost in my memory, whatever stream, river, or ocean I might wade."

## Transitions

The first sentence of every paragraph after the first plays the important role of transitioning. An essay without good transitions is like a series of isolated islands; the reader will struggle to get from one point to the next. Use transitions like bridges between your ideas.

As you move from one paragraph to the next, you should not have to explain your story in addition to telling it. If the transitions between paragraphs require explanation, your essay is either too large in scope or does not flow logically. A good transition statement will straddle the line between the two paragraphs.

The transition into the final paragraph is especially critical. If the reader does not clearly see how you arrived at this final idea, you have either shoehorned a conclusion into the outline or your outline lacks focus. You should not have to think too much about consciously constructing transition sentences. If the concepts in your outline follow and build on one another naturally, transitions will practically write themselves. To make sure that you are not forcing your transitions, try to refrain from using words like *however, nevertheless*, and *furthermore.*

If you are having trouble transitioning between paragraphs or are trying to force a transition on to a paragraph you have already written, you may have a problem with your essay's structure. If you suspect this to be the case, go back to your original outline. Make sure that you have assigned only one point to each paragraph and that each point naturally follows the preceding one, leading to a logical conclusion. This may result in a kind of back to the drawing board restructuring, but try not to get frustrated. This happens to even the most seasoned writers and is a normal part of the writing process.

## Word Choice

Well-structured outlines, paragraphs, and transitions are all important parts of creating a solid essay. However, structure is not everything. An essay can be very well organized with balanced paragraphs and smooth transitions and still come across as dull and uninspired. You know from Chapter 1 that details are integral to interesting essays. Although adding detail is certainly a good start, you need to know more about the kind of writing that holds a reader's attention. First, word choice is very important.

### Rule #1: Put your thesaurus away

Using a thesaurus will not make you look smarter. It will only make you look like you are trying to look smarter.

### Rule #2: Focus on verbs

Keep adjectives to a minimum. Pumping your sentences full of adjectives and adverbs is not the same thing as adding detail or color. Adjectives and adverbs add description, but verbs add action. Action is always more interesting than description.

One of the admissions officers on our panel advises using the following test to gauge the strength of your word choice.

## The Verb Test

Choose a paragraph from your essay, and make a list of every verb you have used. Compare your list to one of the following:

| COLUMN 1 | COLUMN 2 |
|---|---|
| said | has met |
| contorted | can say |
| complain | know |
| learned | are usually |
| spreading | may have heard |
| sprang | are |
| strained | is |
| gripped | strive |
| had been living | may not be involved |
| had attended | try to perform |

These are lists of the first ten verbs found in two of the essays in this book. One was taken from one of the highest-ranked essays in our group, the other from one of the lowest. Can you guess which is which? The essays were not being graded on verb use, obviously. Yet the correlation between strong verbs and high scores is undeniable. Think of it this way: If you had to choose an essay based solely on the verb list, which one would you rather read?

## Sentence Length

Sentence length is very important. Short sentences can be effective, but excessive use of them can make your essay seem choppy. If you tend to write short sentences, make sure you have provided enough detail to make your essay interesting. Long sentences are equally risky. Though they often provide the most detail, sentences that are excessively long can be difficult for the reader to digest. Most admissions officers will give your essay only one shot, so finding the right balance is very important. Reading your essay aloud will usually give you a good indication of whether you have used too many short sentences (frequent pauses) or exceedingly long sentences (gasping for air between one period and the next).

## Beginnings and Endings

Beginnings and endings can be the most challenging part of crafting any piece of writing—and also, in many ways, the most important. Part of the reason that they are so difficult is that writers tend to worry about them too much. So much hype surrounds the necessity of thoroughly introducing the subject and ending with sharply drawn conclusions that anxious essayists compensate by going overboard. They feel that in order to appear mature and worldly, their essays must contain profound insights and sweeping observations.

Do not fall into this trap! One of the biggest complaints that our admissions officers voiced were essayists who tried to say too much in their introductions. "Just tell the story!" wrote one officer repeatedly in response to numerous essays.

Our book contains many examples of good essays crippled by bad beginnings. Look, for example, at some of these introductions and what admissions officers had to say about them:

### Introduction 1

*Of the many ironies which exist in life, one stands out in my mind: the same information which you would like to attain from others if often the same knowledge they would least like to divulge. As competition continues to grow in all areas, many who strive for an advantage must act tactfully and follow Polonius's advice in Hamlet that states, "By indirections find directions out" (II, i, L. 65). A perfect example comes to mind. (Essay 53)*

### Admissions' Comments:

An entertaining story, but the beginning is very awkward, even pretentious. This is a simple story that needs a simple style of writing. The author is trying too hard to impress.

This essay begins with an awkwardly written pseudo-profundity. "What the heck is he talking about?" is my immediate reaction.

I can do without the gratuitous quote from Hamlet. Please! The question was not, "How many intellectual push-ups can you do?" It would have been much better to begin with his brother's pleading. Like this: "Where is it?" my brother yelled. But, I wouldn't answer. "Where is it?" he screamed. I made a dash for the door, but he cut me off, threw me to the floor and landed on top of me. Placing a question at the beginning of an essay is a great hook for catching the reader's attention.

Machiavelli aside, the student takes too long to get to the story.

## Introduction 2

*I am learning, both through observations and first-hand experiences, that there are many mishaps in life which seem to be unexplainable and unfair, and yet have devastating consequences. Disease fits into this category. Its atrocity does not stem from the fact that it is a rare or uncommon occurrence, since illness and disease pervade our lives as we hear numerous stories of sick people and come into contact with them each day. However, there is a marked difference between reading in the newspaper that a famous rock star or sports icon has tested H.I.V. positive and discovering that your own mother has been diagnosed with cancer.*

## Admissions' Comments:

I wish this kid had started the essay with his mom sitting him down in the rocking chair. That would have been a powerful beginning. In general, using the introduction of the essay to paint a scene or mood can be very effective.

Interestingly enough, both these essays would have been greatly improved had the writers simply eliminated their introductions altogether. This is true in a surprising number of cases.

## What? No Introduction?

Do yourself a favor and forget about beginnings and endings during the first stages of writing. Instead of crafting your introductory paragraph first, just write down in your own words, for yourself only, the main point or points that you are going to try to convey in your essay. They should not be grand or worldly. Simple and specific is better. It may be as simple as "prove that I have teamwork skills because of the time I took the blame at soccer practice" or "explain that I am different now from four years ago because I learned to rely on others during my Outward Bound trip." Then dive straight into the body of the essay, starting with your first point.

This technique works because when you have finished writing the rest of your rough draft, you may discover that you do not need an introduction at all. Isn't that risky? Maybe. Believe it or not, though, more essays have been ruined by forced and unnecessary introductions than by the lack of one. This largely occurs because many do not know what an introduction is supposed to accomplish.

This is especially true if you are writing your essay as a narrative. It might feel risky or uncomfortable just letting the story stand on its own. You might be afraid that your reader will miss the point. However, you should make the point in the story—through telling it—not before or after it. If you really cannot resist, then do what Essayist 34 does and offer your observations and explanations in the conclusion instead of the introduction. This leaves you free to begin your essay with the action.

## To Title or Not to Title

Some of the essayists in this book decided to add a title to their essay, although most did not. Essay 48 begins, "The Key to Medical Advancement," and Essay 4 begins, "One Memorable Sailing Practice." Our favorite is the tongue-in-cheek title introducing the humorous essay "On the Eighth Day, God Created No-Trump?" Admissions committees definitely do not require titles. If you are wondering whether or not to add one to yours, remember the old adage, when in doubt, leave it out.

## Leading the Way

The most important part of any beginning is, of course, the lead. Leads play the dual role of setting the theme of your essay and engaging the reader. The introduction should not be overly formal. You do not want an admissions officer to start reading your essay and think, "Here we go again." Although admissions officers will try to give the entire essay a fair reading, they are only human. If you lose them after the first sentence, the rest of your essay will not get the attention it deserves.

Just as you should not worry about your introduction until you have gotten an initial draft on paper, you should not begin the writing process by writing the lead. Often, you will spot the lead floating around in the middle of your first draft of the essay. A couple of the essayists in this book missed great lead opportunities by burying the most interesting sentences in the middle of their essays. A good example of this can be found in Essay 48. He begins with the sweeping and impersonal statement, "Throughout the twentieth century, virtually every aspect of modern medicine has reaped the rewards of technological advancements." He made a big mistake! We know that admissions officers want to learn about you in the essay—they are not interested in modern medicine and technological advancements. The writer should have begun with a sentence that he buried in the middle of his third paragraph, "Five years ago, a brain tumor destroyed my brother's pituitary gland."

A good lead does not have to be this shocking to be effective. You can write many different kinds of effective leads. The following lists examples of some of them.

## Standard Lead

Standard leads are the most common leads used. A typical standard lead answers one or more of the six basic questions: who, what, when, where, why, and how. They give the reader an idea of what to expect. A summary lead is a standard lead that answers most of these questions in one sentence. Perhaps the most standard of all standard leads is the one that simply rephrases the question asked. The problem with this kind of lead is that, although it is a logical beginning, it can be dull. The advantage is that it sets your reader up for a focused and well-structured essay. If you live up to that expectation, the impact of your points is heightened. Standard leads are also useful for short essays when you need to get to the point quickly.

*Of all the characters that I've "met" through books and movies, two stand out as people that I most want to emulate.* (Essay 28)

*I am most interested in a career in psychoneuroimmunology. (Essay 4)*

*I have learned a great many things from participating in varsity football. (Essay 2)*

## Creative Lead

This lead attempts to add interest by being obtuse or funny. It can leave you wondering what the essay will be about or make you smile.

*If you like storms that clear a path of change and arcs that bridge communication gaps, slide down my rainbow into the whirlwind of my life.* (Essay 40)

*It is weird being a high school bridge player in Lincoln, Nebraska.* (Essay 41)

## Action Lead

This lead takes the reader into the middle of a piece of action. It is perfect for short essays where space needs to be conserved or for narrative essays that begin with a story.

*Struck with sudden panic, I hastily flipped through the many papers in my travel folder until I spotted the ticket.* (Essay 39)

*Reluctantly smearing sunblock over every exposed inch of my fifty-three pound body, I prepared mentally for the arduous task that lay ahead of me.* (Essay 34)

*A faint twinge of excitement floated through my body that night.* (Essay 38)

## Personal or Revealing Lead

This lead reveals something about the writer. It is always in the first person and usually takes an informal, conversational tone.

*For some reason, my parents felt the necessity to inundate me at a young age with extracurricular activities.* (Essay 3)

*Ever since I was little, I've had this overwhelming desire to travel the world.* (Essay 37)

*It's not that I'm a weak guy, just that I had been somewhat self-conscious about my strength early on in my high school career.* (Essay 19)

## Quotation Lead

This type of lead can be a direct quotation or a paraphrase. It is most effective when the quote you choose is unusual, funny, or obscure and it should not be too long. Choose a quote with a meaning you plan to reveal to the reader as the essay progresses. Some admissions officers caution against using this kind of lead because it can seem like you are trying to impress them or sound smart. Do not use a proverb or cliché, and do not interpret the quote in your essay. The admissions committee is more interested in how you respond to it and what that response says about you.

*Within his poem, "Sailing to Byzantium", William Butler Yeats speaks of escaping from the natural world to a land of paradise.* (Essay 5)

*A Greek philosopher once said, "In argument, truth is born."* (Essay 6)

## Dialogue Lead

This lead takes the reader into a conversation. It can take the form of an actual dialogue between two people or can simply be a snippet of personal thought.

*What are your intellectual interests?*

*Well, gee. I don't really know.* (Essay 5)

*"Je deteste des Americains," said the old Swiss woman sitting across from me.*

## Closing Your Case

The final sentence or two of your essay is also critical. It must finish your thought or assertion, and it is an important part of creating a positive and memorable image. Endings are the last experience an admissions officer has with your essay, so you need to make those words and thoughts count. A standard close merely summarizes the main points you have made. However, you should not feel obligated to tie everything up into a neat bow. The essay can conclude with some ambiguity, if appropriate, as long as it offers insights.

If you have introduced a clever or unusual thought in the first paragraph, try referring back to it in your conclusion. You want the admissions officer to leave your essay thinking, "That was a satisfying read," and "I wish the applicant had written more."

Essay 35, for example, closes with:

*Perhaps, one day, many years from now, a weary young seeker will venture through a thick tangle of vegetation to be welcomed by the roar of a shimmering cataract. Within the shadows formed by the play of sunlight on a cascade of water, will be an old man, bent with age, sitting with feet crossed; the light in his eyes undimmed with the passage of time. And the old man will speak of his own voyage to Byzantium.*

The reference to Byzantium in the last sentence ties back to the first:

*Within his poem, "Sailing to Byzantium", William Butler Yeats speaks of escaping from the natural world to a land of paradise.*

This stylistic touch wraps up the essay nicely. It shows that the writer spent time planning and structuring.

Some last sentences aim to get a laugh, and others present a single, strong image. Some of the admissions officers' favorites from the essays in this book follow:

*I had everything I'd ever need. I was no longer doubting myself among strangers; I was making music with friends.* (Essay 39)

*Understanding my queerness has become a process, a process of deciding that my difference will no longer isolate, relegate, or alienate me. Instead, it will build me a space from which I can expose the perversity in calling someone perverse.* (Essay 31)

*Only now, some of my dreams are finally starting to come true as I live vicariously through the ink of my foreign friends.* (Essay 47)

*Plus I learned two things. One: I can pride myself on the smallest triviality. Two: I'm glad we don't measure strength in our gym classes with the bench press.* (Essay 49)

## Take a Break!

You have made it through the first draft, and you deserve a reward for the hard work—take a break! Let your draft sit for a couple of days. You need to distance yourself from the piece so you can gain objectivity. Writing can be an emotional and exhausting process, particularly when you write about yourself and your experiences. After you finish your first draft, you may think a bit too highly of your efforts—or you may be too harsh. Both extremes are probably inaccurate. Once you have let your work sit for a while, you will be better able to take the next (and final!) step presented in Chapter 6: "Make It Perfect."

CHAPTER 6

# Make It Perfect

---

### Chapter Highlights

Focus only on substance in your first revision.

Read the essay out loud to someone else, and find out if others think it's interesting.

Make sure the essay answers the question.

Carefully scrutinize your word choices.

Consider changing any passages written in passive voice to active voice.

Ensure that the essay flows logically and seamlessly.

Proofread for grammatical errors, spelling mistakes, typos, and so on.

Get feedback!

---

Writing is not a one-time act. Writing is a process. Memorable writing comes more from rewriting than it does from the first draft. By rewriting, you will improve your essay—guaranteed. No perfect amount of drafts will ensure a great essay. However, you will eventually reach a point when the thoughts of others reinforce your confidence in the strength of your writing. If you skimp on the rewriting process, you significantly reduce the chances that your essay will be as good as it could be. Do not take that chance. The following steps show you how to take your essay from rough to remarkable.

## Revise

Once you have taken a break away from your essay, come back and read it with a fresh perspective. Analyze it as objectively as possible based on the following three components: substance, structure, and interest. Do not worry yet about surface errors and spelling mistakes; focus instead on the larger issues. Be prepared to find some significant problems with your essays. Be willing to address them even though it might mean significantly more work. Also, if you find yourself unable to iron out the bugs that turn up, you should be willing to consider starting one or two of your essays from scratch, potentially with a new topic. Use the following checklists to critique the various parts of your essays.

## Substance

Substance refers to the content of your essay and the message you send out. It can be very hard to gauge in your own writing. One good way to make sure that you are saying what you think you are saying is to write down, briefly and in your own words, the general idea of your message. Then remove the introduction and conclusion from your essay and have an objective reader review what is left. Ask that person what he thinks is the general idea of your message. Compare the two statements to see how similar they are. This can be especially helpful if you wrote a narrative. It will help to make sure that you are communicating your points in the story.

Here are some more questions to ask regarding content:

- Have you answered the question asked?

- Do you back up each point that you make with an example?

- Have you used concrete and personal examples?

- Have you been specific? Go on a generalities hunt. Turn the generalities into specifics.

- Is the essay about you? (The answer should be Yes!)

- What does it say about you? Try making a list of all the words you have used to describe yourself (directly or indirectly). Does the list accurately represent you?

- Does the writing sound like you? Is it personal and informal rather than uptight or stiff?

- Read your introduction. Is it personal and written in your own voice? If it is general or makes any broad claims, then have someone proofread your essay once without it. Did they notice that it was missing? If the essay can stand on its own without the introduction, then consider removing it permanently.

## Interest

Many people think only of mechanics when they revise and rewrite their compositions. As we know, though, the interest factor is crucial in keeping the admissions officers reading and remembering your essay. Look at your essay with the interest equation in mind: personal + specific = interesting. Answer the following:

- Is the opening paragraph personal? Do you start with action or an image?
- At what point does your essay really begin? Try to delete all the sentences before that point.
- Does the essay show rather than tell? Use details whenever possible to create images.
- Did you use any words that you would not use in a conversation?
- Have you used an active voice? (See more about this below.)
- Did you do the verb check (see Chapter 5)? Did you use active and interesting verbs?
- Have you overused adjectives and adverbs?
- Have you eliminated trite expressions and clichés?
- Does the essay sound interesting to you? If it bores you, it will bore others.
- Will the ending give the reader a sense of completeness? Does the last sentence sound like the last sentence?

## Structure

To check the overall structure of your essay, do a first-sentence check. Write down the first sentence of every paragraph in order. Read through them one after another, and ask the following:

- Would someone who was reading only these sentences still understand exactly what you are trying to say?
- Do the first sentences express all of your main points?
- Do the thoughts flow naturally, or do they seem to skip around or come out of left field?

Now go back to your essay as a whole and ask these:
- Does each paragraph stick to the thought that was introduced in the first sentence?
- Does a piece of evidence support each point? How well does the evidence support the point?
- Is each paragraph of roughly the same length? When you step back and squint at your essay, do they look balanced on the page? If one is significantly longer than the rest, you are probably trying to squeeze more than one thought into it.

- Does your conclusion draw naturally from the previous paragraphs?
- Have you varied the length and structure of your sentences?

## The Hunt for Red Flags

How can you know if you are writing in passive or active voice? Certain words and phrases are red flags for the passive voice. Relying on them too heavily will considerably weaken an otherwise good essay. To find out if your essay suffers from passivity, hunt for all of the following, highlighting each one as you find it:

| | |
|---|---|
| really | rather |
| there is | it is important to note that |
| it is essential that | however |
| nonetheless/nevertheless | in addition |
| in conclusion | for instance |
| yet | very |
| although | in fact |
| I feel | I believe |
| I hope | can be |
| maybe | perhaps |
| usually | may/may not |
| have had | somewhat |

When you are done, how much of your essay have you highlighted? You do not need to eliminate these phrases completely, but ask yourself if you need each one. Try replacing the phrase with a stronger one.

## Proofread

When you are satisfied with the structure and content of your essay, it is time to check for grammar, spelling, typos, and the like. You can fix obvious things right away: a misspelled or misused word, a seemingly endless sentence, or improper punctuation. Keep rewriting until your words say what you want them to say. Ask yourself these questions:

- Did I punctuate correctly?
- Did I eliminate exclamation points (except in dialogue)?
- Did I use capitalization clearly and consistently?
- Do the subjects agree in number with the verbs?
- Did I place the periods and commas inside the quotation marks?

- Did I keep contractions to a minimum? Do apostrophes appear in the right places?
- Did I replace the name of the proper school for each new application?

## Read It Out Loud

To help you polish the essay even further, read it out loud. You will be amazed at the faulty grammar and awkward language that your ears can detect. This will also give you a good sense of the flow of the piece and will alert you to anything that sounds too abrupt or out of place. Good writing, like good music, has a certain rhythm. How does your essay sound? Is it interesting and varied or drawn out and monotonous? This is also a good way to catch errors that your eyes might otherwise skim over while reading silently.

## Get Feedback

We have mentioned this point many times throughout this text but can never emphasize it enough: Get feedback! Not only will it help you see your essay objectively, as others will see it, but it is also a good way to get reinspired when you feel yourself burning out.

You should have already found someone to proof for general style, structure, and content as Chapter 1 advised. If you have to write multiple essays for one school, have that person evaluate the set as a whole. As a final step before submitting your application, find someone new to proof for the surface errors that only fresh eyes will see. Give the proofreader this book and have that person check off the questions as he or she proofs.

As said earlier, if you are having trouble finding someone willing (and able) to dedicate the time and thought that needs to be put in to make this step effective, you may want to consider getting a professional evaluation. In addition to our Web site (*www.ivyessays.com*), a number of qualified services can be found on the Internet.

## Sad but True: Real Essay Gaffes

You would be amazed at the things that get written in admissions essays—even at the top schools. The following is a list of some of the funniest mistakes found by the admissions officers on our team. Remember that behind the hilarity of these errors lurks a serious message: Always proofread your essays! Otherwise, you will get the same reaction that these other applicants did: "It makes you wonder if these kids care about their essays at all," said one of our staff. "I never know whether to call it apathy or ignorance," said another, "but either way, the impression is not good." Then again, at least they got a laugh!

- Mt. Elgon National Park is well known for its rich deposits of herds of elephants.

- I enjoyed my bondage with the family and especially with their mule, Jake.

- The book was very entertaining, even though it was about a dull subject, World War II.

- I would love to attend a college where the foundation was built upon women.

- The worst experience that I have probably ever had to go through emotionally was when other members of PETA (People for the Ethical Treatment of Animals) and I went to Pennsylvania for their annual pigeon shooting.

- He was a modest man with an unbelievable ego.

- Scuba One members are volunteers, but that never stops them from trying to save someone's life.

- Hemingway includes no modern terminology in *A Farewell to Arms*. This, of course, is due to that fact that it was not written recently.

- I am proud to be able to say that I have sustained from the use of drugs, alcohol and tobacco products.

- I've been a strong advocate of the abomination of drunk driving.

- If Homer's primary view of mortal life could be expressed in a word it would be this: life is fleeting.

- Such things as divorces, separations, and annulments greatly reduce the need for adultery to be committed.

- It is rewarding to hear when some of these prisoners I have fought for are released, yet triumphant when others are executed.

- Playing the saxophone lets me develop technique and skill which will help me in the future, since I would like to become a doctor.

- However, many students would not be able to emerge from the same situation unscrewed.

- I look at each stage as a challenge, and an adventure, and as another experience on my step ladder of life.

- "Bare your cross," something I have heard all my life.

- There was one man in particular who caught my attention. He was a tiny man with ridiculously features all of which, with the exception of his nose, seemed to drown in the mass of the delicate transparent pinkish flesh that cascaded from his forehead and flowed over the collar of his tuxedo and the edge of his bow tie.

- Take Wordsworth, for example; every one of his words is worth a hundred words.

- For almost all involved in these stories, premature burial has had a negative effect on their lives.

- I know that as we age, we tend to forget the bricklayers of our lives.

- I would like to see my own ignorance wither into enlightenment.

- Another activity I take personally is my church Youth Group.

- The outdoors is two dimensional, challenging my physical and mental capabilities.

- Going to school in your wonderfully gothic setting would be an exciting challenge.

- My mother worked hard to provide me with whatever I needed in my life, a good home, a fairly stale family and a wonderful education.

- I hope to provide in turn, a self motivated, confident, and capable individual to add to the reputation of Vasser University whose name stands up for itself. [Note: the correct spelling is Vassar].

- Filled with Victorian furniture and beautiful antique fixtures, even at that age I was amazed.

- They eagerly and happily took our bags, welcomed us in English, and quickly drove us out of the airport.

- Do I shake the hand that has always bitten me?

- In the spring, people were literally exploding outside.

- Freedom of speech is the ointment which sets us free.

- I first was exposed through a friend who attends [school].

- As an extra, we even saw Elizabeth Taylor's home, which had a bridge attaching it to the home across the street.

- *Under Activities:* Volunteer (Retarded totor)

- *Name of Activity:* Cook and serve homeless

- *On a transcript:* AP Englash

- *Misspelled abbreviation on another transcript:* COMP CRAP (computer graphics)

- *Handwritten on an interview form under Academic Interests:* Writting.

PART FOUR

# Essays, Graded and Ranked

The authors of this book believe that the best way to get inspired and learn how to write a winning essay is to read through examples of essays that have worked in the past. While understanding that not all essays that worked are of the same quality, we wanted to separate the truly outstanding from the ones that were simply good enough.

Whether or not an essay is *good* is subjective, to some extent. Assuming that most of the qualities that make an application essay effective are in place, how well any particular essay is received will depend upon the reader. To provide you with the most helpful and relevant insight possible, we gathered a panel of five admissions officers and had them assign letter grades (A through F) to 25 anonymous essays. When they finished, we tallied all the grades and averaged them to determine the score that you see listed next to each one. In addition, the admissions staff were instructed to explain the specific reasons behind their assessments. What made the A essays so good? What could the writers of the C essays have done to make them better? You will find the results of this exercise in the pages that follow.

The essays found here (and throughout the rest of the book) are not samples; they are real essays written by candidates who were accepted to the top schools. All mistakes, typos, grammar errors, and spelling errors found in the original essays have been preserved. The school that each essay was written for (and to which the essayist was accepted) is listed next to the essay number along with some tags to help you quickly identify the essays that will be most relevant to you. An index to these essays as well as to the essays presented in the rest of this book can be found at the end of this section.

## The Top Ten

The essays in this section were the top scorers of the group. These are the essays that went beyond simply "working"—each one is an outstanding example of its type. To understand what made them so popular with the admissions officers, read the reactions and comments included beneath each essay.

### ESSAY 31: Harvard, personal identity: Asian, Gay Activist
**Score: 95**

Increasingly, I find that I'd much rather talk about queerness than write about it. I don't feel comfortable enough with my words to trust how they frame, limit, and structure my experience. I've yet to notice the experiences for which I have words and those for which I don't. I also wonder how adeptly I can tease out my sexuality anyway, how well I can place it at center, since my particular queerness has had everything to do with my Asianness and uppermiddleclassness and youth. Again, I've yet to learn how to discuss these weaves in tandem, but I will.

Living behind the Orange Curtain, I feel that my sexuality has grounded me outside society. I remember encountering lust during early childhood. I think his name was John, and he was in sixth grade. It seems like my desires have always been there; I simply did not acknowledge them, at first, as particularly interesting or, more tellingly, substantial enough to construct a name, a category, or identity around. My identity remained based in far more conventional structures: although I knew I liked boys, I still expected to become a successful heterosexual doctor, find a dutiful Asian bride, and have an obscene number of children. Sexual orientation, unlike money, racial authenticity, and status, had yet to become a foundation upon which my life rested. Masculinity and sexuality had yet to emerge as an issue.

Gradually, I began to realize that my peers were treating me differently. I wish there was a fresh way to describe alienation, how painful it is to feel like an absolute freak, how name-calling and insults cannot be dismissed as "teasing," how children relish in making people suffer, but such coming-of-age melodramas become trite, even laughable. I remember them mocking me for innocent hand gestures; I remember beginning to watch myself neurotically for any action that they might construe as effeminate; I remember violence; I remember feeling stiff and stale, like granite, icy, numb, each encounter, each slur and slap laying the blocks, smoothing the mortar of my new, emerging self. From behind the rising walls, I watched them becoming couples and realized that I could never have that easy way, that I could never commune with others without sadness.

My parents only complicated the matter. As traditional Asians, they demanded that I, the eldest son, serve as the tantamount heterosexual, a role model for my brothers, the carrier of the potent seed that would foster the next Chiu generation. Soon I learned that the identity they had built for me not only stood on wealth and cultural and familial loyalties, but around virility and manliness as well. I had been obedient for my entire life, willing to fulfill every expectation. Now I faced disownment. I was terrified; I had lost my sense of direction, false or otherwise. As I grew aware of my Otherness, I began to see my life as a series of illusions. My prospects dissolved, and from these mirages emerged barriers, bastions I had never recognized.

Because what I had always considered natural was now wrong, I was framed as the unacceptable, the deviant. Silently, insidiously, the world had reified a Self for me, cemented my most intimate and meaningful desires into an identity of Pervert. It had warped me into a suffocating, totalizing essence, pinned me with the girders of weakness, monstrosity, and leprosy that supported their dichotomous construction of Homosexual. I couldn't let myself stay a freak, so I decided I didn't know who I really was and attempted to redefine myself. First I went ascetic, soaking myself in Buddhism to extinguish my desires, to tear down the source of my aberrant nature. My peers, however, would not let me go so easily. Seeing as they had already decided that my sexuality was my self, I then decided to seek solace with fellow perverts. So, I came out.

Coming out, I was told, would solve all of my problems. Sure, there would still be the leering, the homophobic slurs, and all that, but I would at least be "proud" of my sexual preference; I would "stand up and be counted." In reality, my momentous coming out was anti-climactic and disappointing. I expected that by telling people that I was gay I would metamorphose into a braver, stronger being. I didn't. To a certain extent, I never rested deeply in the closet anyway; because of my "flamboyance," my private and public lives never seemed genuinely partitioned or obscured from one another. For me, at least, the closet emerged as another strange edifice, another harsh, warped, and dichotomous lens through which to understand myself.

Consequently I returned to my original foundations, plunging into schoolwork to redeem myself through academic excellence. Still miserable, I turned to extracurricular activities and community service, trying to erect an identity in a facade of social responsibility and activism. I found myself searching for the approval of others. Their praise of my right image, my unperverted, correctly structured image—my stellar transcript, my hours of community service, my ability to blow into a flute and scratch out a few greeting card poems—reassured me of my worth. Despite the rigidity of my A-student identity, I still felt stale and numb, dizzy and nauseous, my body floating in black and crimson. My life was nothing but a series of unstable illusions, shadows that consumed and rejected me, a society that told me that, beneath any self I pieced together, my sexuality made me essentially perverse and nothing more.

I reject these ideas. As Foucault writes, queerness represents a constructed, implanted perversity. People see my sexuality as the defining aspect of my persona. They see it as the sum product of my past and the determining factor of my future. Everywhere people limit me in ways far more insidious than stereotyping or anti-gay legislation. Discrimination against gays and lesbians is not simply a homophobic don't ask don't tell policy: in the contemporary consciousness, homophobia builds queerness into a monolith. With queer individuals reduced to nothing but absolutely, impregnably Queer, dehumanization becomes almost inevitable. There are the obvious examples: the gay bashers, the skinhead neo-Nazis, Jesse Helms, those who decry us as Satanic. Yet with the "gay-friendly" we become perverse too, metamorphosing from devils to ABBA-loving fashion freaks. Even queers sometimes yell too thoughtlessly for gay pride, as if having a sexual preference is something of which to be proud. Sexuality is not an accomplishment; it is not something that reveals who you are; it is not all that you are: it exists as a strand, one interwoven into all the other facets of Self.

What I want is gay dignity and freedom. I want to integrate my sexuality with all the other weaves of my self: burn any architectural plans that mount my gayness above my race, ethnicity, and age. In fact, I'd like to trash any designs on fixing my identity at all. I want for people not to trap me, totalize me in predetermined roles and lifestyles, to tell me that I have to resolve my deviance when they have constructed it for me. With horror, I know that I've lived my sexuality with relative ease, that I've passed through high school relatively unbruised, that I've always been able to wrap my Harvard successes around me like a shawl and beat my enemies back with my résumé. Still I am tired of fearing that I might lose my parents' support and never being able to return home after college. I am tired of wondering if a potential employer finds me too effeminate or if I need to carry mace on-campus. I am tired of having my sexuality dominate me, suffocate me, be my persona.

Of course, I certainly can't take it for granted either. For many years, I've distanced myself from certain queers, naming drag queens, transsexuals, and flaming gay activists as freaks or Other to bolster my sense of normalcy. Only recently did I become a crusading warrior princess myself. Gradually, I am coming to embrace the identity of Homosexual, the identity built so rigidly around my desire and so oppressive to my sense of self, and encourage others to do the same. Screw normalcy. Only through reappropriating this artificial category of Queerness we can name ourselves as a community. Only through political mobilization can we reclaim what it means to live Gay, bring our multiplicity as individuals to light, and achieve equity in our lives. Coming out means avowal, a desperately needed acknowledgment of yourself and your peers and a commitment to fight for them: not necessarily a collision of the theoretically public and private. Queers need to proclaim their supposedly perverse subculture, a subculture borne in the oppression, resistance, and struggle within and between the queer and straight communities. We must seek equity through visibility. Moreover, while our identities may remain socially constructed, their fabrication does not make them any less meaningful or real. Perhaps because I can afford to, I have learned to take pleasure in deviance, in flaunting my self; in reveling in sexual experiences; in passing as a girl or heterosexual boy. Certainly my experiences prove as legitimate as the construction of Straightness. We need to establish queerness as just as normal and "unnatural" as Heterosexual convention. We must understand that barbie doll cheerleader is just as contrived as the diesel dyke, that the muscle-bound jock is as much of a construct as the leather queen. Only after achieving a visible place in society and showing Straights how society has fabricated their identities as well will queers move from the deviant to the normal, from the periphery to the center.

So in looking toward my activism at Harvard, I perceive two emerging strands. First, I will continue to work on the numerous issues that I've pursued during high school because in doing so I do justice to all aspects of my self and serve all of my communities. Beyond my attempt to unify and integrate the weaves of my life, I would, however, like to become more present in the Gay, Lesbian, Bisexual, and Transgender community, particularly since my home life and county of residence have largely curtailed my efforts. Despite the importance of the cause, I would definitely like to move beyond A.I.D.S. activism and attack broader social justice issues on sexuality that receive less attention. My human rights work promises to redouble in the area of sexuality as the international human rights community grows increasingly aware of the torture and oppression of sexual minorities worldwide. Moreover, I would also like to study and pursue the creation of alliances within queer communities, in terms of varying racial-ethnic and gender groups, and with heterosexual communities as well. Specifically, however, I feel drawn to the study and teaching of identity politics, particularly in how the social discourse constructs Homo and Hetero-sexuals. I feel a need to collapse the shaky dichotomy between Straights and Freaks, to demolish the structures we've erected to define ourselves. Understanding my queerness has become a process, a process of deciding that my difference will no longer isolate, relegate, or alienate me. Instead, it will build me a space from which I can expose the perversity in calling someone perverse.

**Comments**

This essay was the hands-down favorite of our panel. One admissions officer called it a "work of art," and another described it as "the stuff of graduate research." One admissions officer offered a warning to applicants, though. "This is not the conversational style that I recommend that most applicants use, because too often students at this stage sound pretentious and awkward if they try to go beyond a simple style." Another felt it very important to stress that a topic does not need to be this grandiose, personal, or revealing to be effective. "True, these topics often tug at the heartstrings and therefore get more notice . . . but it's worth mentioning that you don't need to be a gay Asian activist to get noticed."

I would not hesitate to pass this essay along for reading to those friends and loved ones I believe could be helped or moved by it.

This is a work of art. It is the sort of writing I feel incompetent to comment about.

The reasoning and logic of the piece is extremely mature and sophisticated . . . [and] the use of language is masterful.

An incredible exercise in introspection. After reading the essay, I feel like I know exactly what makes this kid tick. Plus, the themes of multiple identities—homosexual, Asian, male—are incredibly mature—the stuff of graduate research, actually.

The author takes a courageous risk in being so completely honest about his sexual orientation in an essay for college admission.

I would welcome the addition of a student who could bring such a well-reasoned point of view to the incoming class.

The combination of such a deeply personal topic, the depth of insight, and the ability to articulate such a breadth of thought is impressive.

## ESSAY 32: Harvard, international experience: Living in Switzerland
### Score: 95

"Je deteste des Americains," said the old Swiss woman sitting across from me. Her face contorted into a grimace of disgust as she and her friend continued to complain that Americans had no culture, that they never learned another language, and that their inferior customs were spreading throughout Europe like an infectious disease. Each hair on the back of my neck sprang to attention, as I strained to hear the women's inflammatory remarks. I gripped my bag of McDonald's harder with each insulting phrase.

I had been living in Geneva, Switzerland for four years, during which time I had attended an international school consisting of over 96 different nationalities. I had already become fluent in French and had become accustomed to the new culture in which I was living—a culture which I had believed to be rich in tolerance and acceptance. Naturally, the women's remarks hurt. Was I really an "ugly American?" Did I have no appreciation of anything other than McDonald's or Coca-Cola? Had I not been touched by the new world I had been exposed to?

Without question, my four years in Switzerland changed my life in countless ways. From the minute I stepped off the plane at Cointrin Airport, the vastly different sights along the clean street, the ubiquitous smells of rich delicious French cuisine, and my feelings of excitement about my new surroundings told me that I definitely was "not in Kansas anymore." My school helped greatly in modifying my attitudes, as for the first time I was with peers from countries which I had only read about. Although it was sometimes difficult trying to find links between my self and my Saudi Arabian, Hungarian, French, Nigerian, or Chilean friends, I soon came to enjoy my new stir fry environment. By the time I left, I was wondering how I ever could survive the boredom of attending a homogeneous institution. This is not to say that, prior to this, I had been closed up in a bland box of a world. I had traveled to India, my father's home, and England, my mother's home, annually: a practice my family and I continue to this day. I had been brought up without specific religious beliefs, but an awareness of my parents' spiritual backgrounds of Judaism and Hinduism. Thus my exposure to these various different nationalities in Switzerland built on my foundations of cultural awareness, rather than laying the cornerstone for it.

My understanding of my new environment was aided tremendously by my ability to speak French, and was subsequently one of the best gifts I brought back from my four year stay in Switzerland. An entire year of school lessons could not have taught me as much of the language as I learned form speaking with my Swiss friends, shopping in the local stores, or apologizing to my neighbors for hitting my ball into their yard. My proficiency in French earned me a regular spot on a nationally broadcast Swiss radio program, in which a Russian child and I discussed tensions between major world powers. This was a rare opportunity, as, although Stephen and I were peers, the fact that Russian children attended the Soviet Embassy school meant that we were not classmates. Though, even if we had been allowed to speak casually before, I am not certain that our conversation would have reached the depth of discussion we achieved on the show.

America will never again seem the same to me. Geneva gave me enough distance to look at my country through objective eyes. Traveling throughout Europe was like a trip with Gulliver: it gave me the ability to look inside myself and discern my country's faults as well as its numerous strengths. Like the Swiss women's remarks, it hurt me to find that the United States is not the only country in the world with a rich and stimulating environment. With my new perspective, I saw that America was not what it had been. Then I thought for a moment and realized that America had not changed, but I had.

## Comments

This essay, though very different from the last, tied with it for first place. One officer called this, "A good example of a foreign culture essay that works." The only negative comments about this essay came from one officer who found the conclusion to be a bit weak. "I would like to see her elaborate a little more in the last paragraph. This is because in most of her classes, she will be required to support any opinions." Another agreed that she could have kept her final points more personal and specific.

The writing is excellent.

The vocabulary is sophisticated without seeming labored. I do not suspect that the author had a thesaurus at hand! This tells me that she/he would certainly be successful academically, at least in the courses that require strong communication and analytical abilities.

This essay is very well written. The writer demonstrates a refreshing maturity that seems to come from his/her abroad experience. The essay demonstrates a transformation of the student from just an American in a foreign land to someone who embraces the international experience and grew with it.

What I like about this essay is that it shows that the traditional categories of "extracurricular activities" need not be the only way to demonstrate that one has something of interest to bring to the college experience. I think this writer would be a fascinating person to get to know, because she would be able to contribute a fresh perspective to conversations about many of the important ideas that we wrestle with in college. She might well be someone who would be especially adept at bringing together diverse members of the student body because she would not feel intimidated by differences, but would, instead, seek them out and value them highly.

## ESSAY 33: Stanford and Amherst, hobbies and interests: Philosophy

Score: 90

Often I lie awake in my bed at night, not moving, too exhausted even to read. The ceiling fan turns slowly overhead, the sheets are smooth and comfortable, and the house lies in the quiet stillness of night, yet I do not sleep. For hours, I am lost in contemplation, my mind incessantly weaving threads of thought together in strange patterns. I silently drift in the darkness through a landscape of intangible ideas, groping for meaning behind the shadow of existence. What is it to be? I have spent years with this question, privately turning it over, searching for its nature, for the form of its answer. I have truly been haunted by Being.

Thus philosophy for me was at first a personal matter, a dream that forced its way into my head during the night. The thoughts arose as from a vacuum, unprovoked, and persisted in their senseless hold over my mind. Yet slowly I learned that others had faced these same questions, that they had spent their lives searching for the answers, and that, most importantly, they had left a written record of their search for meaning. Great minds throughout history had left a legacy which I could follow, turning my insoluble reflections into a legitimate, potentially life-long exploration. As time permitted, I studied philosophy, reading whatever I could find, and my quest for the nature of Being took on a more tangible presence.

Last year I joined the Humanities Forum, a program in which philosophy professors from Emory University and other Atlanta area colleges offer informal courses on a variety of themes. The classes permitted me to make a more systematic and rewarding study than my private readings allowed. Each class meets for two hours once a week, and is composed of undergraduate students, graduate students, and professionals from virtually every field. I am the youngest participant. I began the program with a twelve-week course called "Our Civilization," with primary readings from Alexis de Tocqueville, Adam Smith, and Friedrich Nietzsche, in which we evaluated what modern culture has lost in comparison to ancient Greek and medieval value systems and social structures. Later, in "Plato vs. Descartes: Ancient and Modern Philosophy," we explored the distinctive natures of the two philosophical eras by examining the thought of an influential thinker from each period. I am currently enrolled in "Heidegger, Metaphysics, and Nihilism." We are examining Heidegger's thesis that nihilism is the culmination of Western metaphysics by reading and discussing a variety of his works. Heidegger is the most profound thinker I have encountered; I often find myself forced to reread passages to grasp the meaning hidden within. In Heidegger, I have found the closest approach to the truth of Being, the truth I still contemplate alone at night.

Occasionally I come upon a familiar concept in my philosophical reading, one which I recognize as my own. To see my private musings, which seemed only ephemeral and abstract, expressed in the writings of a great thinker excites me to pure exhilaration. That this elusive creature Being has haunted others gives me hope; I now look forward to the setting of the sun and the sleepless night ahead.

## Comments

Most of our panel admired this essay for its passion and depth of thought. One officer cautions, however, that "it is the very depth of the author's passion about these ideas that would prompt me to be very careful about my decision about this applicant. If he were applying for a program in philosophy then this essay would be completely appropriate . . . [but] if he truly does spend countless sleepless hours worrying about the Big Questions, I wonder if he will be a bit too highly strung for the pressures of college life. Will he be able stay calm and centered when the pressures of homework and exams begin to build?" By and large, though, this essay was a definite "yes!"

Wow. This is a virtuoso. This essay is intelligent, creative, thoughtful, descriptive, humble, and interesting. There's a saying among coaches that applies here: "You can't coach speed." You can't teach this kind of writing.

The author is obviously a profound thinker, well beyond his years in his grasp of deep philosophical ideas. He writes with intelligence and sophistication about concepts that many of his peers seldom even consider.

## ESSAY 34: Princeton, childhood experience: A Fishing Trip
Score: 88.8

Reluctantly smearing sunblock over every exposed inch of my fifty-three pound body, I prepared mentally for the arduous task that lay ahead of me. After several miserable fishing ventures which had left my skin red and my hook bare, I felt certain that, at last, my day had arrived. I stood ready to clear the first hurdle of manhood, triumph over fish. At the age of seven, I was confident that my rugged, strapping body could conquer any obstacle. Pity the fish that would become the woeful object of the first demonstration of my male prowess.

Engaging me deeply was my naive eagerness to traverse the chasm dividing boy from man. In fact, so completely absorbed was I in my thoughts that the lengthy journey to our favorite fishing spot seemed fleeting. The sudden break in the droning of the engine snapped me to reality. Abruptly jarred back into the world, I fumbled for my fishing pole. Dangling the humble rods end over the edge of the boat, I released the bail on the reel and plunked the cheap plastic lure into the water. Once I had let out enough line and set the rod in a holder, I sat back to wait for an attack on the lure. The low hum of the motor at trolling speed only added to my anxiety, like the instrumental accompaniment to a horror film. And then it hit. A sharp tug on the line pulled me to my feet faster than an electric shock. I bounded to the pole, and when I reached it, I yanked it out of the holder with all of my might. My nervous energy was so potent that when I tugged on the rod, I nearly plunged headlong over the side of the boat and into the fishs domain. Although adrenaline streamed through my veins, after five minutes both my unvanquishable strength and my superhuman will were waning steadily. Just when I was fully prepared to surrender to the fish and, with that gesture, succumb to a life of discontentment, pain, and sorrow, the fish performed a miraculous feat. Shocked and instantly revived, I watched as the mahi-mahi leapt from the oceans surface. The mahi-mahis skin gleamed with radiant hues of blue, green, and yellow in a breathtaking spray of surf. Brilliant sunlight beamed upon the spectacle, giving life to a scene which exploded into a furious spectrum of color. The exotic fish tumbled majestically back to the sea amidst a blast of foam. With this incredible display, the fish was transformed from a pitiful victim to a brilliant specimen of life. I cared no longer for any transcendent ritual I must perform, but rather, I longed only for the possession of such a proud creature. I hungered to touch such a wonder and share the fantastic bond that a hunter must feel for his kill. I needed to have that fish at any cost.

The fight lasted for only ten minutes; nevertheless, it was a ten minutes which I will never forget. When my fish neared the boat, I felt more energized than I had when the fish first struck. At my fathers command, I netted the fish and hauled it into the bottom of the boat. I was nearly bursting with exhilaration.

Released from the net, the fish dropped to the bottom of the boat with a hollow thud, and my jaw dropped with it. I stared in complete horror at the violently thrashing fish which was now at my feet. Within minutes, all of the fishs vibrance, color and life had vanished. Instead, came blood. Lots of blood. It sprayed from its mouth. It sprayed from its gills. Shortly, the boat was coated with the red life blood of the mahi-mahi. It now lay twitching helplessly while it gasped and choked for oxygen in the dry air. I felt sickened, disgusted, and utterly lost in heart-wrenching pity. As I watched the color drain from the fish, leaving it a morbid pale-yellow, I realized that I was responsible for the transformation of a creature of brilliance and life into a pitiful, dying beast.

Despite my brothers cheers and praises, I rode back to shore in bitter silence. I could not help thinking about the vast difference between the magnificent creature which I saw jump in the sea and the pathetic beast which I saw gasping for life in the bloody pit of the boat. What struck me most forcefully on that day, though, was the realization that I was no mere bystander to this desecration. I was the sole cause. Had I not dropped the hook into the water, the fish undoubtedly would still be alive. I, alone, had killed this fish.

In retrospect, I am relieved that I reacted in such a way to my passage from boyhood to manhood. Although my views about many things, hunting and fishing included, have changed considerably since that day, I still retain a powerful conscience which actively molds my personality. One cannot dispute the frightening potential of the human race to induce the permanent extinction of every life form on the planet. As the ability to change the world on a global scale is arguably limited to one breed of life, so, too, is the force which impedes instinctual and conscious action, the human conscience. My own sense of strong moral principle reaches far beyond simply averting Armageddon, however. I often find myself unable to disregard this force of moral and social responsibility in whatever I do. Part of my keen social conscience is demonstrated in the effort I have made to be a positive intellectual leader among my classmates and in the community. Realizing how lucky I am to have been born with a high aptitude for learning, I feel sorry that others who also work very hard cannot achieve like I have nor be rewarded with success as I have been. In a leadership role, I hope to constructively guide my peers to find their own success and see the fruition of their own goals. By serving as class president for three consecutive years, as founder, member, and chairman of the peer counseling society, and as a peer tutor, I have enabled others to reach their goals, while finding personal gratification at the same time. I am fortunate in that I have been given the opportunity to optimize the usefulness of my personal virtues in helping others; I can only hope to continue heeding my conscience in work as a research chemist, or whatever I may do in the future. It is my right and my obligation, for I firmly maintain that the charge of a humanitarian conscience is one which each person must eternally bear for the good of humankind and all the world.

## Comments

Our panel loved the personal touch of this essay. "A good example of how a talented writer can make a standard topic appealing" was the general consensus. One officer did think, though, that the writer got "overzealous" with his language and could have avoided some of the more corpulent sentences like, "Engaging me deeply was my naive eagerness to traverse the chasm dividing boy from man," by writing with a simpler, more natural voice.

I really enjoyed this essay. It starts with a wonderful, humorous touch, but describes vividly and movingly the young boy's first experience with death and with personal responsibility.

In reading this essay, I get a strong impression of the kind of person this young man must be, someone full of good humor, but great sensitivity as well. His

117

easy way with the language convinces me that he would be an excellent student, and a welcome addition to the class.

This was a nicely written piece. This student took time to think about this experience and was able to articulate his memories of his fishing adventure rather well. This could have been another bland essay but the writer took you on the adventure with him, from boyhood to manhood.

I like the way he took his fishing adventure and transitioned to his life today and how and what he learned from it.

What I liked most about the essay was that the writer told of an experience in his childhood and was able to take that experience and make the connection to his life and goals of today.

## ESSAY 35: Yale, funny/creative: Showering
### Score: 87

Within his poem, "Sailing to Byzantium", William Butler Yeats speaks of escaping from the natural world to a land of paradise. Indeed, we all have a place we go to in times of need, whether it be for consolation, comfort, or thought. Aristotle had his Lyceum, Caesar his Forum, Buddha his Bo tree. And I, [name], I have my shower.

It is here, under the shiny brass and cheap plastic, under the delightful stream of golden ambrosia, that I, [name], frisbee player and philosopher extraordinaire, have planned my life's accomplishments. For, like the Oracle of Apollo, the showerhead tells no lies. Within my shower, soap and water are united as one. They are Yin and Yang, the shower is the Tao, and more.

In four years of high school, the shower has never failed me yet. With its bright lighting and adjacent mirror, I am forced to literally look myself in the eye. It is in the shower, under a calming spray of water, that I realize when I have been at fault. For unlike the world outside, the shower forces me to confront myself. And in doing so, I have made some of the most important decisions in my life.

It was in the shower, two years and three months ago, when I realized for the first time that eating as much as my 320 pound speech coach had given me love handles. A moment later, realization became panic. But the shower is more than a place of revelation; it is a place of contemplation as well. The cooling influence of the water soon calmed me, and I thought of joining cross-country. And in the months to follow, it would be the stark shape of my excess blubber which would haunt and propel me to greater efforts until I earned my Varsity Letter that very first year.

Cross-country is not the only form of athletics to have its roots in my shower. Four years of summer studies at Duke University had taught me to love Ultimate Frisbee. One summer, when I had grown too old to return, it was the shower which provided my solution. Standing under the showerhead, it suddenly dawned on me that I should found my own Ultimate Frisbee Club at school. Thanks to a shower, the Ultimate Frisbee Club of [school] has become one of 22 schools in California to play the sport.

And yet, the shower is much more than merely a place of instantaneous revelation, it is also a proving ground for old ideas and practices. Unknown to the rest of Monte Vista Speech and Debate, it is the shower which is my very essence. In four years of debating, my coaches have grown accustomed to getting calls late at night about a new argument for the team. I have my old coach to thank for my initial success in extemporaneous speech. However, after his departure, I have realized that giving practice speeches to myself in front of that all-revealing mirror is at as least large a reason for my continued success. To look my coach in the eye and try to get away with skewed analysis on "The Effect Privatization of Ecuador's Industries will have on its Economy" is one matter. But, to try to lie to myself in that mirror is yet another.

My shower is my morality. Not only can I not get away with excess flab on my waist, but I cannot hide from my self either. The bright lights and the mirror reveal more than the physical body. Looking into my own eyes, into my own soul, I see what a careful observer would see. All my good traits and my flaws appear, a synthesis of light and dark, molding itself into the grey of reality. To lie to that person, would be to deny all that I am. And thus, the shower has become the purest reflection of me. Were I to have enclosed a picture of myself, it would not have had more meaning.

Perhaps, one day, many years from now, a weary young seeker will venture through a thick tangle of vegetation to be welcomed by the roar of a shimmering cataract. Within the shadows formed by the play of sunlight on a cascade of water, will be an old man, bent with age, sitting with feet crossed; the light in his eyes undimmed with the passage of time. And the old man will speak of his own voyage to Byzantium.

## Comments

This is a good example of making an essay creative and memorable with an unusual topic choice. Our panel appreciated the humor and tongue-in-cheek approach this writer took. The major drawback mentioned was that this essay is "a perfect example of a FAILURE TO PROOFREAD! There are misspellings, run-on sentences, and comma errors throughout the text. These are careless mistakes which are easily avoidable, and consequently they diminish the strength of the essay." Another officer felt that the last paragraph was confusing and took itself too seriously, which "diminishes the effect of the essay."

A well-written essay. The writer has a unique spin on inner reflection. It was an enjoyable essay to read because it really gave you a sense of how this young person thinks and has evolved. It also illustrated how everyone is different when it comes to the process of inner reflection. A refreshing outlook.

The shower metaphor is a delightful and offbeat approach to the rather serious topics of personal growth and improvement. The author obviously is capable of being honest with herself and living up to challenges. I think this person would be a lot of fun to spend four years of college with.

I like this opening: It's a very self-conscious "mountain-out-of-a-molehill" approach.

Nice contrast between the Forum, the Lyceum, and the shower!

Interesting essay. I like the concept of the shower as a place of revelation, both philosophical and physical. The student has dropped many hints about what's important to her—athletics, debate, persistence, honesty—and she has done so in a very unusual way.

I like the way she brings things full circle by ending with a reference to Byzantium; it is a subtle nod to [her] opening sentence, but it provides effective closure.

## ESSAY 36: Carnegie-Mellon, current affairs: Middle East Debate
Score: 86.4

A Greek philosopher once said, "In argument, truth is born." Even though sometimes feelings and emotions come into play that confuse the issue at hand, usually an argument results in a new insight on the subject. Even if a person holds strong views that are unshaken by anything his adversary may say, he may nevertheless gain from the debate. It forces him to organize and analyze his views, leaving him with a clearer understanding of the subject than before. Further, his opponent's arguments help him better appreciate his views and their differences. Finally, the argument forces both to look inwards, at their character and value system.

For these reasons, I enjoy debating issues that are important to me and about which I hold strong views. One such issue receiving great national attention is the Middle East peace process. While the peace process has always been important to the American community as a whole, and more specifically to the Jewish American community, the assassination of Israel Prime Minister Yitzhak Rabin has focused the spotlight upon it, as well as intensified the debate around it. Since I attend a private Jewish school, I often discuss this topic with my peers, often finding myself in the minority. Most of them support the peace process, while I adhere to the views of the Likud (opposition) party, which opposes the peace process.

Complicating the issue are several emotional stigmas that are often attached to it, transforming the discussion from an objective one to one driven by passion. The foremost of these stigmas is the accusation, which is often hurled at the opponents of the peace process, of promoting war and violence. Often made by people who know little about the issue, this view fails to realize that opposition to the peace process does not imply opposition of peace. Rather, it implies disapproval of certain tactics and specifics of the peace process as it was carried out by Rabin.

Another commonly advanced accusation against American Jews who disagree with the peace process centers around the question of whether they have the right to influence Israeli policy. "You don't have to send your children to the Army," it is said, "your children don't die in wars. What right have you to oppose peace?!" The fallacy of this argument is that it doesn't differentiate between belief and action. While it is true, for precisely the reasons above, that American Jews have no right to try to influence Israeli policy, that does not preclude them from having ideas of what that policy should be.

Finally, the assassination of Yitzhak Rabin has introduced yet another dimension into this debate. In its aftermath, opposing the peace process sometimes is identified with condoning the assassination itself. Such an identification of the man and his beliefs involves grave dangers, such as rashly implementing his ideas in a flurry of compassion and commiseration.

What all of these stigmas have in common is that they forsake logical and objective debate, opting rather for emotions, generalizations and accusations. And the dangers of that happening are the main lesson I learned from my debates. While those debates have shed new light on the issue and have forced me to reconsider what I think is moral and just, most importantly they have demonstrated the necessity of objectiveness and removal of emotions from the discussion, especially when, as in the case of the peace process, thousands of lives are at stake. When passions and hatred take over, we must stop and think of what it all is really about.

## Comments

The social concerns or ethics essay is notoriously difficult to write. This essayist tackles it well with solid arguments, clear thinking, and good structure. The main suggestion for improvement came from one officer who felt that the statements made in the first paragraph were too broad and lofty for a college essay.

Very clear headed.

This student put time and energy into this essay and it shows in the writing style, the flow of discourse, and the conclusions that the writer comes to in the end. It is a well thought out essay with depth and focus.

This essay is well written, and brings out an interesting point of view, one of which I had not been aware until now. This author grasps the subtleties of a difficult political position. I think he would be an interesting person to know, and would certainly make people think, both in class and in discussions outside of academics.

The argument in the essay is logical and substantiated with solid examples, making it an effective representation of the student's thought and writing style while revealing the student's personal opinions on the Middle East peace process.

## ESSAY 37: Harvard, international experience: A Visit to Kenya
### Score: 85.6

**A Visit to Rural Kenya**

At the end of July, after my freshman year of high school, I boarded a plane that would take me from my home in Cincinnati, Ohio, to Nairobi, Kenya. My parents had always wanted to take our family abroad, but when my mother signed a contract to work for the U.S. Agency for International Development in Kenya, plans materialized, and we were soon on our way to an exotic year in Africa.

Besides the farewells I had to make to my friends at home, I had few reservations about living abroad. What made it easy for me to come to Africa was my eagerness to immerse myself in a new culture. I knew that I might never get such an experience again, so I was determined to learn all I could about the language, the history, and the people, of that far-off place.

During the first few months of our stay, my family took various trips around the country. We watched zebra and wildebeest migrate across the Serengeti, saw hippos floating like rocks in Lake Victoria, marveled at flamingos balancing knee-deep in a salt-lake. We climbed an extinct volcano in the Rift Valley. We snorkeled in the Indian Ocean and fed fish from our fingers. We hiked 17,000 feet above sea level to the peak of Mt. Kenya. And we studied Swahili, the local language, every evening after dinner. But in late October my aunt came to visit for a month.

She romanced us with stories of her experiences in rural Africa working in the Peace Corps. The sharp contrast between the simple lifestyle she described and the one I was leading shocked me as to how un-African my life was. I went to an American school every day with mostly Europeans and Asians, which, despite being a unique experience itself, isolated me from the larger Kenyan community. I was also living in a city, where shopping malls, Italian restaurants, late-night discos, and movie theaters were all available close at hand. Was this really what I had come to see? My daily activities were almost the same as the ones in the United States. I typed English essays late at night on a computer; I showered with hot water every day after soccer practice; I dined on fried chicken or fish fillets or hamburgers. I was in the midst of a swarm of expatriates who had formed a community so tight that I could live with all the luxuries of a technologically-modern lifestyle. I saw my problem: I had wound myself so tightly in the routine of my school life that I was no longer seeing Kenya or even Kenyans. I yearned to know some of the African culture, but I didn't know how that could be achieved without a drastic break in my academic progress, which I wasn't willing to sacrifice.

After talking over this issue with my parents, I stumbled upon the perfect solution. [name] is the son of [name] and [name], with whom my mother lived twenty years ago when she came to Kenya as a volunteer nurse. [name] was living with us while he attended [name] College, but he was going back to his home village to visit his family over the Christmas holidays. I could go with him and stay with his family there.

This excursion proved to be the most rewarding ten days of my entire stay in Africa. In that short period, I learned more about Kenyan culture than I had in the five months prior to that time. First of all, I witnessed how different the female role is in Kenya than in America. The women— young and old—did about twice the work the men did. They had to cook the meals, get the milk, sweep the house, chop the firewood, take care of the children; the list goes on and on. The men did some work on the farm, but mostly they enjoyed a laid-back lifestyle. And it is not uncommon for a man to have more than one wife. [Name] has had a total of three women as wives. What seems unheard-of to a Westerner is commonplace to a Kenyan.

I also saw an intense restlessness for change. When the men sat around the dinner table (women weren't allowed to eat with them), they would not merely discuss the weather or the latest gossip of the village. No, they debated the problems and merits of Kenya and what could be done to improve their country. They voiced their apprehension of the government, their fear that if they openly opposed the established authority, their family could be persecuted by the president's special agents. They talked of the A.I.D.S. epidemic spreading through the

123

working class like wildfire. They expressed their anger at the drug abuse of their nation's youth. But these men were unwilling to accept the obstacles they faced and instead looked toward solutions—education, fairer elections, less corruption, and others. I also saw that a primitive life is not necessarily a painful one. Theirs is a simple life—one without running water, or electricity, or telephones, or cars. But being simple did not mean it was a pleasureless life. It meant fetching water every day from a well. It meant cooking over a fire and reading by a lantern. It meant walking to school instead of driving. But it also meant no expensive phone bills, no wallet-straining car repairs, no broken washing machines. A simple life had its hardships, but it also avoided the hassles that Americans face in their complex modern lives. In the village, we ate good food, children screamed and shouted with joy, we laughed while playing card games, we flipped through old photo albums. Their lifestyle was vastly different from mine, but they still had the same goals that I did: to have fun, to get a good education, to be comfortable. After the New Year, when I returned to my home in Nairobi, I went back carrying in my mind a vivid picture of rural Kenya, but also satisfied that I had learned something that could not be found in Nairobi's American expatriate community.

## Comments

This essayist benefited from having had an unusual travel experience and from knowing how to write about it using lots of colorful detail. Two officers mentioned that the writer could have improved the essay by making her conclusion more reflective. "What do these things mean?" asked one. "In the conclusion, the all-important self-reflection is absent. . . . Remember, if you want to write an essay about your immersion in a foreign culture, you must be able to articulate how you've grown from the experience; a mere recounting of events is not enough."

This is very well written. I especially like the vivid descriptions of the African scenes. It shows us a young woman who is extremely open to new experiences, who wants to immerse herself completely in whatever new situation comes her way. She would be a valuable addition to an entering class.

Solid all-around essay from beginning to end. This is one of those essays that you hope more students would write. This student knows what it takes to compose a quality essay. It is told in an expressive way that allows you to envision the experience yourself. Excellent form and writing. This student has a keen sense for details and how to tell a story. EXCELLENT.

## ESSAY 38: Brown, achievement: Martial Arts Competition
Score: 83.6

A faint twinge of excitement floated through my body that night. A hint of anticipation of the coming day could not be suppressed; yet to be overcome with anxiety would not do at all. I arduously forced those pernicious thoughts from seeping in and overcoming my body and mind. I still wonder that I slept at all that night.

But I did. I slept soundly and comfortably as those nervous deliberations crept into my defenseless, unsuspecting mind, pilfering my calm composure. When I awoke refreshed, I found my mind swarming with jumbled exhilaration. The adrenaline was flowing already.

After a quick breakfast, I pulled some of my gear together and headed out. The car ride of two hours seemed only a few moments as I struggled to reinstate order in my chaotic consciousness and focus my mind on the day before me. My thoughts drifted to the indistinct shadows of my memory.

My opponent's name was John Doe. There were other competitors at the tournament, but they had never posed any threat to my title. For as long as I had competed in this tournament, I had easily taken the black belt championship in my division. John, however, was the most phenomenal martial artist I had ever had the honor of witnessing at my young age of thirteen. And he was in my division. Although he was the same rank, age, size, and weight as I, he surpassed me in almost every aspect of our training. His feet were lightning, and his hands were virtually invisible in their agile swiftness. He wielded the power of a bear while appearing no larger than I. His form and techniques were executed with near perfection. Although I had never defeated his flawlessness before, victory did not seem unattainable. For even though he was extraordinary, he was not much more talented than I. I am not saying that he was not skilled or even that he was not more skilled than I, for he most certainly was, but just not much more than I. I still had one hope, however little, of vanquishing this incredible adversary, for John had one weakness: he was lazy. He didn't enjoy practicing long hours or working hard. He didn't have to. Nevertheless, I had found my passage to triumph.

My mind raced even farther back to all my other failures. I must admit that my record was not very impressive. Never before had I completed anything. I played soccer. I quit. I was a Cub Scout. I quit. I played trumpet. I quit. Karate was all I had left. The championship meant so much because I had never persevered with anything else.

In the last months, I had trained with unearthly stamina and determination. I had focused all my energies into practicing for this sole aspiration. Every day of the week I trained. Every evening, I could be found kicking, blocking, and punching at an imaginary opponent in my room. Hours of constant drilling had improved my techniques and speed. All my techniques were ingrained to the point where they were instinctive. Days and weeks passed too swiftly. . . .

I was abruptly jolted back into the present. The car was pulling into the parking lot. The tournament had too quickly arrived, and I still did not feel prepared for the trial which I was to confront. I stepped out of the car into the bright morning sun, and with my equipment bag in hand, walked into the towering building.

The day was a blur. After warming up and stretching, I sat down on the cold wooden floor, closed my eyes, and focused. I cleared my mind of every thought, every worry, and every insecurity. When I opened my eyes, every sense and nerve had become sharp and attentive, every motion finely tuned and deliberate.

The preliminary rounds were quiet and painless, and the championship fight was suddenly before me. I could see that John looked as calm and as confident as ever. Adrenaline raced through my body as I stepped into the ring. We bowed to each other and to the instructor, and the match began.

I apologize, but I do not recall most of the fight. I do faintly remember that when time ran out the score was tied, and we were forced to go into Sudden Death: whoever scored the next point would win. That, however, I do recall.

I was tired. The grueling two points that I had won already had not been enough. I needed one more before I could taste triumph. I was determined to win, though I had little energy remaining. John appeared unfazed, but I couldn't allow him to discourage me. I focused my entire being, my entire consciousness, on overcoming this invincible nemesis. I charged. All my strenuous training, every molecule in my body, every last drop of desire was directed, concentrated on that single purpose as I exploded through his defenses and drove a solitary fist to its mark.

I was not aware that I would never fight John again, but I would not have cared. Never before had I held this prize in my hands, but through pure, salty sweat and vicious determination, the achievement that I had desired so dearly and which meant so much to me was mine at last. This was the first time that I had ever really made a notable accomplishment in anything. This one experience, this one instant, changed me forever. That day I found self-confidence and discovered that perseverance yields its own sweet fruit. That day a sense of invincibility permeated the air. Mountains were nothing. The sun wasn't so bright and brilliant anymore. For a moment, I was the best.

## Comments

The admissions officers admired this essay for its passion and sincerity. In fact, most of the noted drawbacks were based on the writer being too passionate. "Kind of a tempest in a teapot, don't you think?" wrote one. Other suggestions for improvement were "purely editorial" such as the overuse of adjectives and adverbs, using a passive voice, and making contradictory statements. "For example, he says, 'I slept soundly and comfortably as those nervous deliberations crept into my defenseless, unsuspecting mind, pilfering my calm composure.' How could he sleep soundly and comfortably if the nervous deliberations were pilfering his calm composure? There are a few other examples like that that I won't go into here. I would just suggest that the author look carefully to be sure his ideas stay consistent and support one another."

What I like about this essay from the point of view of an admission officer is that I am convinced that the change in attitude described by the author is real. I do believe that he will carry with him forever the hard-won knowledge that he can attain his goals, that perseverance and hard work will eventually allow him to succeed in any endeavor. This is an important quality to bring to the college experience. Especially when considering applications to prestigious institutions, the admission committee will want to feel sure that the applicants understand the need for hard work and perseverance. Many times the strongest-looking applicants are students for whom academic success has come so easily that the challenges of college come as a shock. I always like hearing stories like this, of students who know what it means to struggle and finally succeed.

## ESSAY 39: Harvard, hobbies and interests: Violin
### Score: 83

Struck with sudden panic, I hastily flipped through the many papers in my travel folder until I spotted the ticket. I nervously thrust it toward the beaming stewardess, but took the time to return her wide smile. Before stepping into the caterpillar tunnel I looked back at my parents, seeking reassurance, but I sensed from their plastered-on grins and overly enthusiastic waves that they were more terrified than I. I gave them a departing wave, grabbed my violin case, and commenced my first solitary journey.

Seated in the plane I began to study the pieces I would soon be performing, trying to dispel the flutterings in my stomach. I listened to some professional recordings on my Walkman, mimicking the fingerings with my left hand while watching the sheet music.

"Where ya goin'?" smiling businessman-seatmate interrupted.

"To the National High School Orchestra," I answered politely, wanting to go back to the music. "It's composed of students chosen from each state's All-State ensemble." After three days of rehearsal, the orchestra would be giving a concert at a convention center in Cincinnati. I focused back on the music, thinking only of the seating audition I would have to face in a few hours.

When I arrived at the hotel in Cincinnati, instruments and suitcases cluttered every hallway, other kids milled around aimlessly, and the line to pick up room keys was infinitely long. In line I met my social security blanket, a friendly Japanese exchange student, [name], who announced proudly and frequently, "I fro Tayx-aas!" Both glad to have met someone, we adopted each other as friends of circumstance, and touched on a few of the many differences between Japanese and American culture (including plumbing apparatuses!)

Soon all of the performers received an audition schedule, and we went rushing to our rooms to practice. I had an hour until my audition, and repeated the hardest passages ad nauseam. When my time finally came, I flew up to the ninth floor and into the dreaded audition room. Three judges sat before a table. They chatted with me, futilely attempting to calm me. All too soon they resumed serious expressions, and told me which sections to perform. They were not the most difficult ones, but inevitably my hands shook and sweated and my mind wandered. . . .

I felt giddy leaving the audition room. The immense anxiety over the audition was relieved, yet the adrenaline still rushed through me. I wanted to yell and laugh and jump around and be completely silly, for my long-awaited evaluation was over. After dinner the seating list would be posted and I would know just where I fit in with the other musicians, all of whom intimidated me by their mere presence at the convention.

Solitary, having been unable to find [name] or any of my three roommates, I entered the dining room. I glanced feverishly around the giant room which swarmed with strangers.

I gathered up all of my courage and pride for the first time ever, and approached a group I had no preconceived notions about. I sat quietly at first, gathering as much information as I could about the new people. Were they friend material? After careful observation of their socialization, I hypothesized that these complete strangers were very bright and easy to talk to, and shared my buoyant (but sometimes timid), sense of humor. I began to feel at home as we joked about S.A.T.'s, drivers' licenses, and other teenage concerns. I realized then how easy it is to get along with people I meet by coincidence. I became eager to test my newfound revelation.

The flutterings returned to my stomach when I approached the seating lists which everyone strained to see. "I knew it; I got last chair," I heard someone announce. My flutterings intensified. I located the violin list and scanned for my name from the bottom up. My tender ego wouldn't let me start at the top and get increasingly disappointed as I read farther and farther down. "There I am, seventh seat. Pretty good out of twenty," I thought. . . .

Every day at the convention seemed long, only because we did so many wonderful things. We rehearsed for at least seven hours each day, made numerous outings, and spent time meeting new friends.

On the second day, during a luncheon boat ride on the Ohio River, [name] and I sat together, both dreaming of Japan. Looking over at her as we talked, I remembered that in two days I would be torn from the young, promising friendships I had been building. When some friends—including a few I had met at the dinner table on the first night—approached us, bearing a deck of cards, I became absorbed in a jovial game and quickly forgot my sorrow.

Rehearsals were magical right from the start, because everyone rapidly grew accustomed to the strangely professional sound of the group and began to play without reserve, with full dynamics. I continually gazed, wide-eyed, around the large, bright room, watching others, admiring their skill. We were surrounded by pure talent, and the sky was our limit. We blossomed under the conductor's suggestions, using our pre-developed technique to its fullest.

Each time the orchestra played, my emotion soared, wafted by the beauty and artfulness of the music, bringing goose-bumps to my skin and a joyful feeling to my soul. I felt the power of the group—the talent and strength of each individual—meld into a chorus of heavenly sound. I was just where I wanted to be. I had everything I'd ever need. I was no longer doubting myself among strangers; I was making music with friends.

## Comments

This essay contains a good example of wowing the committee with a good closing sentence. Last lines are usually hard to manage. However, this essayist does a great job with hers, and the panel definitely noticed.

The last sentence of the essay is wonderfully composed.

The last line of this essay captures what I think are the two strong points of this piece. First of all, the author is an accomplished musician. No matter what sort of institution you are applying to, be it a music program, a liberal arts university, or a technical institution, strong musical ability will always be a big plus with the admission committee. This is because they know that proficiency in music requires self-discipline, a desire to improve and a willingness to learn. If you have achieved a notable level of accomplishment in some area of music, and have also succeeded in maintaining good grades, it tells an admission officer that you can manage your time well and set your priorities. The second strong point of this essay is the author's description of how she made friends and became completely immersed in appreciating and enjoying the entire experience. This tells an admission officer that she will almost certainly take to the college experience the same way, that she will overcome initial shyness, throw herself into a new situation, and soon extract every ounce of pleasure and personal growth from the experience. She will certainly be an asset to the incoming class.

Good essay, well written and heartfelt.

This was a nice essay. The writer took her time to formulate her ideas about this experience and was keen to stay focused on telling her story succinctly. She took this very important opportunity in her life and was able to tell the reader a vivid account without overdoing it.

## ESSAY 40: Harvard, personal identity: Feminist
Score: 82.6

If you like storms that clear a path of change and arcs that bridge communication gaps, slide down my rainbow into the whirlwind of my life. In a sense, I'm taking the world by storm. I'm either blessed or cursed with an optimism born not of ignorance, but of idealism based on personal experience. Perhaps foolishly, perhaps not, I believe that enough people in this world care for humanity to lift us out of our downward spiral of poverty, depression, and despair. Caring is just the first step, though. Next, people have to work together to achieve the social reforms necessary for our survival. I have chosen to concentrate my whirlwind energy in the reform of feminism.

Why feminism? The path there was so clear and miraculous that I knew it had to be right:

A voice called her softly. She looked and saw a twisting road with obstacles at every turn. The path of silence she was on was so smooth and safe: no one would ridicule her, ostracize her, or hate her. Why should she switch to the difficult road of social battles and criticism? The voice called again and she knew she must take the twisting path, for herself, her sisters, her mothers, and her daughters to be. "But I'm scared!" she cried to the wind. "We all were at first," a million voices whispered back, and this gave her the strength to take the first step on the winding road. And after the first step, it was easy.

Encouraged by a personal meeting with Gloria Steinem, I decided to start a young feminist club at [name] High School to address issues of gender equality. We organized a feminist assembly to raise consciousness about women's issues and to dispel the myths surrounding feminism. We also held a bake sale to benefit Planned Parenthood, and we participated in many Pro-Choice rallies and marches. I spent much of my free time volunteering for local social activism groups, such as the Marin Abused Women's Services and the San Francisco Chapter of the National Organization for Women.

Other social activities provide experiences in the political and judicial world. My sense of justice and desire for competition drew me to Mock Trial, where I am trained as an attorney and argue a difficult case in front of a real judge. This not only teaches me about the judicial system, but also about my own legal rights. I also enjoy Model United Nations, where we act as delegates from other countries in large conferences modeled after the United Nations. This shows me how the policies that affect this country and others are made.

These are only some of the social activities in which I immerse myself. In addition to these, I love writing. I especially enjoy creative writing, such as plays and poems, and I work as Features Editor on the school paper. I like poems and plays because they're a creative way to express my social views and the school paper lets me explain and illustrate important points to a large number of people. All these activities usually keep me busy. In fact, the only real obstacle to obtaining my high school diploma was my lack of time for academics, due to my involvement in all these exciting activities. I found myself staying up all night to finish homework because I had had a NOW meeting or a campaign phone-banking session during the afternoon and evening!

My various activities have taught me many things. Most importantly, I've learned that one must work to change the world, yet one must also have a sense of humor. Nothing can be taken too seriously, even oneself. Above all, we must always work to help others because that is the only way to truly help ourselves.

## Comments

This is another case where the applicant expressed her passion for the subject well. None of the officers reacted negatively to the creative first half. One, however, admitted, "I was a bit put off by the melodramatic style at first, but I like the young woman's energy and enthusiasm. It is clear that she would be an active contributor to the campus community." The suggestions offered mainly focused on the second half of the essay, which some felt read too much like a list of "what I do with my spare time." Another wished that the writer had focused on telling the story of meeting Gloria Steinem instead.

The overall essay was very well thought out. . . . She was able to articulate her personal discovery of feminism and translate how she has incorporated it into her everyday life.

I thought her essay flowed nicely from her interest in feminism to how she is engaged with her various activities and how she has grown from her high school experience.

I would hesitate a bit over her comment about how all of her activities interfered with her academics. If her transcripts revealed weak grades, I would seriously doubt her ability to manage her time well enough to keep up with the increased demands of college-level academics.

## Mixed Reviews

When we tallied the results of the grades given by our panel of five admissions officers, five essays refused to fall neatly into one group or the other. The reason? The officers on our panel simply could not agree about them. Each one was considered to be very good by at least one officer. In fact, each of the five in this group received at least one A—and believe it or not, each one received at least one D as well. Some literally received a different letter grade from every officer, ending up with a full spectrum from A to F.

Interestingly, essays that evoke a wide range of opinions can benefit the applicant more than the ones that everyone agrees are good. These essays create more controversy than the hands-down winners, and controversy makes an essay more memorable. The five essays in this group, for example, evoked more commentary than essays in either of the other two groups, where there was more consensus.

This does not mean that you should intentionally attempt to write essays that will rouse a range of opinions. It means that you should ultimately write for only one person—yourself. You will never be able to predict accurately how every admissions officer will view your essay, because all of them will view it differently. Just do the best job that you can. Rest assured that the committee will, at the very least, recognize and credit you for the effort.

## ESSAY 41: Harvard, funny/creative: Bridge Player
Score: 82.4

### On the Eighth Day, God Created No-Trump?

It is weird being a high school bridge player in Lincoln, Nebraska. My friends give me strange looks when I interrupt their important football discussions to talk about bidding and play problems. My teachers are equally ignorant of the game. One teacher congratulated me for winning a bridge tournament, and asked how long it took me to build it.

The teacher was surprised when I told her the award was for playing the card game, not for building model bridges.

Is it so peculiar to like a card game? Am I a "nerd" who picked the wrong hobby? Why is it that my heroes in life are Oswald Jacoby, Paul Soloway, and Ely Culbertson, while my friends idolize Michael Jordan or Wade Boggs?

Why is it that my dream vacations consists of going to a beach resort only to stay indoors playing a card game with ladies four times my age?

Why is it that when I go to sleep, I think about the different ways I should have played board number three? Why do I dream of successful bidding sequences while my friends think about sports or girlfriends or why that pimple had to appear?

Why is it that most kids watch T.V. or talk on the phone when they have free time, but I study the difficult details of a triple squeeze, Bath Coup or a thrilling deceptive play?

Why is that when my friends brag about certain shots they made in basketball or a grade they received on their history test, I listen, but when I mention my magnificent bridge play, they daydream?

I do not honestly know the answers to these questions. I am, however, hooked on the game. Each bridge hand is a complicated puzzle. It requires total concentration to solve each one, and the effort and absorption places me in another world. My friends do not know what they are missing.

In order to encourage my friends to play, I started a bridge club at my high school. A local professional and I instructed the club once a week. Sixteen new students learned how to play bridge; five enjoyed the game so much that they are now frequent players at duplicate games. The participants received free bridge T-shirts and books and participated in a local bridge tournament. The bridge club has been on local television and in the newspaper. With time and effort there will be other "nerds" playing cards with me.

## Comments

The appealing quality of this essay is its offbeat topic, which the author sums up nicely in a great opening sentence. Admission officers love to be entertained so the announcement that I am about to encounter the trials and tribulations of a high school bridge player is a nice attention grabber.

There are a couple of things I like about this essay. First of all, the author has a natural, lighthearted style. He doesn't take himself too seriously, but is nevertheless serious about his hobby. Second, it is just interesting to come across someone with an unusual hobby like this.

He would bring something unique to his class.

I like the use of the "whys." Essentially, the student is couching her personal characteristics in probing questions about herself; this is much more interesting than reading, "I admire great bridge players more than great athletes," etc.

The questions go on a bit too long for me. Unfortunately, what starts as a unique essay ends up a pretty standard one. Don't misunderstand: There is nothing inherently wrong with her discussing how she founded the bridge club and sponsored a tournament. But these last two paragraphs lack the punch, creativity, and wry self-deprecation found earlier in the essay.

This is a good essay with a quirky topic (always a plus), but it wouldn't have me bursting into my colleagues' offices shouting, "You've got to read this!"

The essay left me feeling that he's probably a neat kid in a quirky kind of way, but I remain unimpressed overall.

The essayist has a good story to tell. He needs to think a bit more about how to tell it. The rhetorical question that begins paragraphs 3–7 gets tiresome after one use. Especially when his conclusion is, "I do not honestly know the answers to these questions." Then don't waste the reader's time asking them.

The biggest question that I have is why so many two-sentence paragraphs. Students always try to find creative ways of writing college essays. Some succeed but most miss the mark. This one missed the mark. The essay is short, without much depth and really lacks form.

## ESSAY 42: Harvard, hobbies and interests: Science
Score: 81.8

**At this juncture in your life, what would be your ideal career and why?**

I am most interested in a career in psychoneuroimmunology. Scientists who work in this area study the biological connection between the mind and immunological factors relating to health and healing. This is my ideal occupation because it includes my two criteria for a career: I would be doing something to benefit society and performing a job that is enjoyable, challenging and meaningful to me.

Throughout the ages, scholars have tried to find ways to alleviate human pain. Although multitudes of procedures have been tried, none have been completely successful. Drugs can relieve pain temporarily or ease the symptoms of a disease. Antibiotics can cure some illnesses but not every one and not instantaneously. Regardless of the outcome of disease and treatment, the patient may have to endure a great deal of pain. The mind, however, can be a powerful tool. If people could learn to rehabilitate themselves quicker with a positive attitude, we could, on the practical side of things, reduce hospital stays and increase productivity, and, in general, lead longer, happier, and healthier lives. I want to be able to help people ease this possibly unnecessary suffering.

This career promises the type of in-depth medical research combining a multidisciplinary approach that greatly appeals to me. If the neurological or genetic basis for why some people heal faster or more effectively than others could be discovered, then we could develop similar ways to treat others. People who recover faster and more fully from certain diseases than the average person could be studied using a variety of psychological, immunological, and neurological tests in an attempt to detect any unique characteristics they might possess.

Many people have hypotheses about different aspects of this subject, but much more investigation needs to be done before we know anything for certain. I want to be one of the individuals involved in basic research to advance our knowledge in this area. Despite the fact that research on these topics is in its infancy, I am very optimistic for its future impact on human health and well-being. As I look forward to becoming a pioneer in this area, I am prepared for what might be a long and sometimes frustrating search. Yet I also envision groundbreaking discoveries or on a more realistic scale, solving smaller pieces of a larger puzzle which may lead to a long-awaited breakthrough.

I know how difficult and also how rewarding research can be because both of my parents are researchers, and I have done research projects for my science courses. The most important thing, of course, is that humanity may benefit. Such a pursuit of knowledge would be incredibly satisfying because of its potential to help so many. To me, the call to a lifetime of this work is irresistible.

## Comments

This essay was well written and thought-out. The student who wrote this was focused on the topic and went all out to explain his or her ideal career.

The mechanics and form were well done and the reader was able to understand the thought process of the writer and why he has an interest in this career.

This is a solid essay and illustrates the intellectual depth of the writer.

This essay is ultimately rather dull. Very little of the author's personality comes through. I am sure the author will turn out to be a dedicated student, but the essay doesn't convey to me anything about what he will bring to the class.

Yawn. "Reduce hospital stays and increase productivity. . . ." Did I stray into a health insurance seminar? Wake me when it's over, and not a moment before.

## ESSAY 43: Stanford, achievement: Friend with Down's Syndrome
Score: 81.8

Throughout my life, I have had to face few outward travails. On the surface, everything comes easy to me. I have never gone hungry or had any physical challenges. And yet, I have had to overcome many inner obstacles over the years. I have a strong sense of purpose and a morality which binds me rigidly. But, at the same time, I admit that I was born a coward. It has taken years of effort and endurance, goaded by my sense of right and wrong, for me to reach where I am today. And over the years, there have been times where my future character was decided in a conflict between fear and morality.

When I was ten, I was on a swim team which included an eighteen-year-old boy with Down's Syndrome. Because of his slurred speech and other physical handicaps, he was never really an accepted member of the team. At first, his size and physical traits made me afraid of him. But I spoke with my father, and he explained the other boy's problem. It was then I decided to befriend the boy. With time, we became good friends. Surprisingly enough, I found myself in the position of the older boy: putting up with his "childish" antics, tying his shoelaces, and teaching him games.

Half a year went by and we were eventually moved up to the next level, practice times were changed. Unfortunately, on the very first day, there was trouble. The older boys (aged twelve to fifteen) began to make fun of my friend. Although he was physically stronger than the others, my peaceful friend did not know how to deal with the verbal abuse. I was upset but I was also afraid of the older boys. But then, the mocking became physical and my anger overcame my fear. In a heat of rage belying my ten years and frail body, I jumped onto a bench, yelling back. Moments later, I found myself in a hopeless fight against an older boy.

The fight would seal any hopes I had of making myself accepted. Nevertheless, thinking back, the incident still brings tears to my eyes. For a split moment, when he rushed in to save me, I looked into my friend's eyes. And within, I saw something which cannot be fully described in words. It was neither outright gratitude nor a mocking "You shouldn't have done that." But for the first time, I truly understood exactly what he wanted to say.

## Comments

This was very moving. I like the fact that it shows a young man who is self-aware and sensitive. He does not cling rigidly to his first impression of a situation (as when he first met the young man with Down's syndrome), but does what he can to learn more about it and to change his behavior appropriately. This says to me that in the college environment he would keep himself open to new experiences and make every effort to allow himself to grow in response to the new situation.

This is a very good essay by a sensitive and intelligent writer. You hope his kind and thoughtful nature will rub off on his fellow students.

He'd get an A if he were a better technical writer.

Here you have an example of the benefit of just telling the story.

Good effort, but I wish he had made more of his conclusions.

If I had been advising the author before he sent in this essay, I might have suggested that he make the tone just a little less self-deprecating. For example, his statement, "I have a strong sense of purpose and a morality which binds me rigidly. But, at the same time, I admit that I was born a coward," plays against the overall tone of the essay. Unless one is attending a religious institution, one is going to encounter people with a wide variety of value systems. "A morality which binds me rigidly" will concern an admissions committee that is looking to build a class of people who learn from one another. This does not mean that you cannot make it clear that you have your own strong set of values. It just means that you should be careful of the language you use to describe it.

I wonder if the word "travails" in the first sentence was actually the first word that came to the author's mind. It sounded immediately to me as though he had checked a thesaurus for a fancier word than "trials" or "problems," and it sounded unnatural and forced. As a rule, try not to use words that you wouldn't use in normal conversation.

This essay was rather disappointing. It was short and not fully developed. The topic of the essay was interesting but the writer completed the essay without delving into the relationship with the young boy with Down's syndrome. The essay leaves the reader without much to go on. The student could have expanded more about the relationship and how becoming friends with someone with D.S. has affected his perspective on life.

## ESSAY 44: University of Pennsylvania, family illness: Grandmother
Score: 80.4

**You have just completed your 300-page autobiography. Please submit page 217.**

Wisdom—The Definition of [name]
reflection. The image was one of kindness, warmth, love. The silver lines of her hair shimmered in the sunlight, and the pale wrinkled cheeks

smoothed when she smiled. I sat there beaming at her. She sat there smiling at me. Life was simple.

"Beep, Beep, Beep" the machine interrupted. It commanded my attention. Sitting at the side of the bed, my eyes became alert once more, glancing at my grandmother. "Why did this have to happen now? She was recovering from lung cancer. Now, hepatitis too?"

Glancing at her hands made me reminice. Hands that had helped me to reach the ice cream sandwiches my tiny fingers couldn't quite grasp. Hands that had knitted my doll's clothes, my baby blanket, my bright tri-colored scarves. Hands that had come together in prayer at my grandfather's funeral. How many times had I held those hands? I saw the ring in her finger. I remembered the scene earlier, when she had tried to give me the ring, telling me to take it when she passed away. At that time I could see the frightened child in her. She was not ready.

I had been so busy over the years placing urgent over important. I thought of all those letters unwritten, phone calls unmade, and visits forgotten, while I was stressing about tennis matches, homework, and friends. Everything was so trivial.

Looking at her face, I saw the resemblance to my own mother. Imagine the hurt my mom must be going through. Losing a mother is one of the greatest pains in the world, a knife wound to the heart. I remembered the stories of my mother as a child, always asking the unanswerable question and dreaming to be the successful professional. Those were similar to the stories I had also heard about myself. How I longed to hear another story. Reaching out my hand to touch her forehead, I saw her eyelids flutter open, revealing mocha coffee colored eyes that held warmth, sprinkled with sweet love. "Still sharp," I thought to myself.

"We were wrong," the doctors said. All three came into the room to apologize, too happy to be ashamed. "The result turned out to be negative. You don't have. . . ." The man's voice was interrupted by clapping. My grandmother sat there smiling like a young puppy.

## Comments

I absolutely love this essay. I love the sentiment for the grandmother that is so thoughtfully expressed. I love the smooth transitions from the focus on the grandmother, to the writer, to the mom, to the writer, and then concluding with the grandmother. The crisp imagery based on only a few examples perfectly represents each of the three women in the essay. And, perhaps more important than the refined writing is the insight that the essay gives the admission committee about what is really important to the writer: an awareness of the deep value of family and the small details that define it.

This essay is almost completely free of writing errors. In fact, there are only three and they are hardly worth mentioning. The word "reminice" is misspelled and should be "reminisce" and "storied" should be "stories." Also, the writer probably meant to write "the ring on her finger" instead of "the ring in her finger." In all three cases, the mistakes are probably typo errors rather than true misspellings.

I thought the writer did a decent job with the question. The writing is basic but page 217 of the 300-page biography was vivid and left the reader curious about page 218.

Well written, nice use of language—but it doesn't say much of anything!

This is sweet, but I don't know quite what to make of it.

This is rather sentimental and trite, and doesn't tell me a great deal about what the author would contribute to the class. However, it is well written, and I do get the impression that the author would be a pleasant person. The essay would not have a lot of influence, either positive or negative, on my ultimate decision.

## ESSAY 45: Cornell, personal identity: Pragmatic and Idealistic
Score: 78.6

Some say that mankind is complex beyond comprehension. I cannot, of course, speak for every other individual on this earth, but I do not believe that I am a very difficult person to understand. My life is based upon two very simple, sweeping philosophies: pragmatism in actions and idealism in thought. Thus, with these two attitudes, I characterize myself.

Pragmatism in actions. I believe utterly in one of those old cliches: we are given only a limited time upon this earth and every moment wasted is lost forever. Therefore, I do not engage in those things that I view as useless. The next question is obvious. What do I view as useless? In reality, perhaps too many things and definitely too many to address in one essay. However, I can indulge in the discussion of a few. Hate is a wasted emotion. Hate accomplishes nothing. It does not relieve hunger. It does not alleviate pain. It creates only avoidable aggression. I do not believe in any kind of hate, including prejudice and racism. My energies and time can be better spent elsewhere. Anger too. What does anger do? Nothing. It frustrates us and aggravates us, and we can avoid it. Being frustrated is not a pleasing experience for me. When I was young, or rather, when I was younger than I am now, I would explode at the smallest disturbances (I'm sorry mom and dad). Now, I have realized that anger is a waste of time, and I no longer have a temper to lose. I would much rather wallow in happiness. And in my happiness, I do not worry much over my image in the eyes of others. The important word here is much, for there are opinions of certain individuals about which I do care a great deal, but these are few. They include my family, my close friends, and those who possess the power to affect my life significantly (for example, university admissions officers). Otherwise, I pay no attention to whispers behind my back or vague rumors circulating in the air above. As long as I know the truth, however harsh it may be, and those that I care about know the truth, I am not troubled. The masses may think as they wish. They are entitled. As can probably be observed from this essay thus far, my outlook on life saves me more than a bit of stress. I hate no one, I am never angry, and I really don't care what most other people believe. It is quite a calming experience. Have no fear though, stress pierces my existence from many other venues.

And now for the other half of my personality. I am a hardcore idealist (and very naive). I believe that I can change the world, and I intend to. Either one man at a time, or a generation at a time, I will leave my stamp emblazoned upon humanity. I maintain that there lies in man the ability to accomplish anything and everything. Nothing is impossible. But before changing the world, we must learn to change ourselves. And here enters another one of my theories. There are two stages in resolving a problem, and they are both equally important. First, the problem must be identified and recognized. Then, the solution may be found. I know that my profound theory sounds ridiculous and obvious, but many people never even pass the first level. They know something is wrong and they complain, but they do not take the time to divine the source of their troubles. If only they would open their eyes a bit and look around, they might find that the key to their dilemma was actually quite simple. Then again, the answer might be more difficult than the problem itself. Admitting the existence of a problem becomes even more difficult when the issue concerns the self. I am continually striving to improve myself, constantly seeking perfection. I sometimes ask others to critique my personality and my actions and reveal what they regard as my flaws. Then, I can better evaluate myself with their more objective views. After that, the process is not complicated. I identify those areas that I am not completely satisfied with and determine some means to rectify the condition. So far, I have not had many difficulties with this fix-it-yourself, or rather, this fix-yourself-yourself system. This self-improvement has given me self-confidence as well as an optimistic attitude on living. By demonstrating to myself that I alone can change the many aspects of my persona, I have led myself to believe that all aspects of life can be altered as well. All that is required is a bit of will (and some intelligence helps too). I believe the will of man is the greatest driving force in our lives.

So there it is. My entire mentality has been reduced to a two page essay. Here and there it's a bit foolish, but it is what I live by (until, of course, I find better philosophies). Others may accept it or reject it, but I don't mind much either way as long as it works for me.

## Comments

The best part of this essay is the writer's choice of a topic that reflects personal opinion and personal style. In two pages, this student demonstrated writing ability, critical thinking, personal philosophy, personal experiences, and conviction while using a touch of self-deprecating humor to keep it light.

A solid essay. This student lives life as an individual. Nothing seems to stop this student from moving forward in life. This student wants the reader to understand him in a way that the rest of the application would not be able to communicate.

The student puts himself out there and feels comfortable with his beliefs. It is refreshing to find a young person who really wants to be an individual among the hordes of copycats.

The essay is well structured and does a good job of supporting the writer's "two very simple, sweeping philosophies" that are outlined in the introduction.

There are several incidental writing errors that if corrected, could make this already well-done essay even stronger. Common errors such as lack of agreement between singular/plural nouns and pronouns, and mixed verb tenses in the same sentence or paragraph.

This strikes me as aloof. It doesn't really make me like the kid—and that's what a good essay should do!

I found this essay to be trite and pretentious. It really tells me nothing of substance about the author. I have no idea what he will bring to the incoming class, what sorts of interests or activities he has been involved with, what concrete goals he may have. The essay also has a self-righteous feel to it that is annoying.

This essay has a cumbersome beginning. This writer should just drop the first two sentences and begin, "my life is based on . . ." then drop the next sentence, "Thus, with these two attitudes, I characterize myself." No one writes or talks that way; not if they wish for anyone to listen.

The author blusters that he will "change the world." Then give me one concrete example of a change you've already made. Be genuine enough to give the reader a good-faith deposit on your lofty proclamations. As the saying goes, "If you're gonna talk the talk, you better walk the walk."

# Essays That Worked (and How They Could Have Been Even Better)

Each essay in this section is an example of a good essay that the writer could have made even better. Like those students who wrote all the other essays in this book, top schools across the country acccepted the writers of these essays. However, even though all of these essays worked, our panel of admissions officers identified the areas that need improvement. Their comments and suggestions follow each essay.

## ESSAY 46: Harvard, personal identity: Bedroom Tour
Score: 80.6

**You have been asked many questions on this application, all asked by someone else. If you yourself were in a position to ask a thought-provoking and revealing question of college applicants, what would that question be?**

Question: If someone were to look through your bedroom, what do you hope your possessions would convey about you?

A typical teen's room? In some respects, yes, but in many ways, my room has become an extension of my personality, interests and values. Upon entering, one would probably notice the lack of any music group, scantily clad female model, or indeed, any adornment at all on my walls. I prefer the unsoiled look of clean walls, which provide a sense of calm. However, my room is far from military precision and order; my bed lies unmade and yesterday's wardrobe gathers dust on the floor. The visitor may consider my room tidy, but not inflexible.

While touring my room, one would surely stop to look through the room's workspace, my desk and computer. The desktop is fairly organized, consisting of a pencil holder, desk calendar, and assorted textbooks. The calendar is full of important dates—tests, deadlines, and of course, the rare days off from school. Academics are one of my highest priorities, but would be useless without occasional relaxation. Above my desk hangs a bulletin board. Similar to the calendar, it holds important pieces of information, as well as a few personal items. A postcard, a present from my grandfather, would likely catch one's eye. The postcard is from my homeland, and includes a famous quote by Mahatma Gandhi. It reminds me of the country I was born in, and the ties I have to my original culture. Directly below the postcard hang a few baby pictures of myself, mementos of a simpler time. Alongside my desk is a computer, without which I could not survive. The slightly outdated, yet fully competent Apple Macintosh aids with school, and, nearly any other activity I participate in. The Mac also has a modem, connecting me to the global community linked through the Internet. I am very interested in the Internet, and have found it a very useful source of information for everything ranging from tomorrow's weather to buying a new car. Upon leaving my workspace, I hope my possessions would convey that I am serious about my work, but I approach it with practicality and a grain of salt.

On the other side of my room lies my relaxation area, commonly referred to as a bed. Strewn about the bed are two magazines which represent my interests, MacWorld and Time. I read these magazines daily, to keep up with current events as well as advancements in the information age. Atop my bureau lays the latest work by Stephen King. The content may not be as deep and insightful as Jane Austen's or Keats, but his stories serve their purpose in providing light entertainment. The bed is unmade, a fact for which I feel no remorse. Although my mother disapproves, I consider an unmade bed a symbol of rest and quietude. My bed may be considered utilitarian, for its uses are not limited to sleeping upon. Some of my best moments of focus and concentration have occurred while lying on the bed and staring at the ceiling, producing thoughts ranging from T.V. shows to pondering college life. Few teen rooms can be considered complete without a loud stereo and an assorted collection of tapes and C.D.'s. My room is no different—my music collection occupies two shelves. Past the techno-rubble of the Eighties lie my current favorites, alternative rock. If a visitor were to turn on the stereo, he would find a couple presets devoted to "homework" music, classical and light jazz. I find that these sounds provide a sense of tranquillity while trying to do homework, write reports, or complete college essays. My bed and surrounding areas represent my non-academic, more human interests. They personify the activities and hobbies which I truly enjoy, and provide a breather from some of the more rigorous aspects of life.

After exiting my room, I would hope my visitor learned a few important things about me. I consider my academics seriously, and devote much of my time (and room) to them. However, they do not necessarily dominate my existence; loud music and Stephen King novels also play a role.

## Comments

Most of the admissions officers liked the question that the applicant chose to ask himself. "This is one I tell my students to prepare to answer when they go to an interview," says one, "and the writer's response is a good one. He literally brings the question home." "Descriptive and informative," writes another. Although no one felt that this essay was strongly flawed, they made a number of suggestions about how the author could have rewritten the essay to create more of an impact.

The writing style is a little too rigid. The writer should let go of the fear that he won't be taken seriously unless he uses a formal style. The writer should replace stodgy sounding phrases like "while touring my room," with the more straightforward, "as you look around my room." If this were one of my students asking advice, I'd pat him on the back and say, "Lighten up, it's your bedroom. Don't use words like quietude and utilitarian. Relax and have fun with this."

The last paragraph needs to be dropped altogether. If the essay has done it's job, recaps like this are obvious and unnecessary.

This essay does not, unfortunately, convey an impression of a very active person. Whether or not he meant to, I picture the author as someone who spends a lot of time alone in his room playing with his computer and reading lightweight novels. I don't see what he would contribute to campus life. This is something that applicants to technical institutions in particular should be wary of. Admission officers at such places tend to be especially unreceptive to applicants who seem to believe that being a "computer jock" is all the credentials they need for admission.

## ESSAY 47: Chicago, hobbies and interests: Pen-pals
### Score: 80.2

Ever since I was little, I've had this overwhelming desire to travel the world. It seemed I was forever reading Motorland, hoarding travel brochures, and tacking up pictures of the places I wanted to visit all over the walls of my room. It was difficult for me to fathom that there could possibly be people living in faraway places, people who spoke strange languages, who practiced unusual customs, and who had cultures so different from my own. My parents couldn't understand my fascination for these distant places, nor did they share my passion for them. They just thought I was a dreamer, and they were right. I was.

One day when I was flipping through my latest travel magazine, I came across something I had never seen before. It was a page filled with the addresses of kids from all over the world who wanted pen pals! I could barely contain my excitement as I dashed into the kitchen to ask my mother if I could write to one of them. She said, half-paying attention, "Sure, dear, whatever you like," and I bounded happily back to my room. But then I was faced with a dilemma—which one should I write to? So I did what seemed logical at the time, and after eeny-meeny-miny-mo-ing my finger landed on an address from Finland. It belonged to a girl named [name]. . . .

That was the beginning of my first overseas friendship, and there would be many more to come. In one of her letters, [Name] sent me a little booklet called an "FB" or "friendship book." Inside it, many people had scrawled their names, addresses and a few of their hobbies. The idea was to add your name to the FB, write to anyone else you found interesting, and send it along to another one of your pen pals. So I flipped through the FB and wrote my name on a blank page, but having no one else to send it to, I returned it to [Name].

Within a month I received letters from the Philippines and from Austria. I was extremely shocked to be getting mail from people I didn't even know, but nevertheless I was very excited! In the ensuing months I wrote my name in many more FB's, and I continued to get letters from places as far away as Mauritius, Estonia, Korea, Sweden, Germany, Denmark, and Indonesia. Over the years I've become very close to a number of my pen pals, and I can honestly say that some of my best friends live in other countries.

My pen pals are much more than friends, though. They have taught me about their cultures, their politics, and many other things that I never would have learned in school. In a day's mail, I can learn about anything from Maltese cuisine to the collapse of the pearl industry in Bahrain to the various slang words used by teenagers in England (although I still don't know what "fanned" means). What I learn is not only interesting, but may prove to be invaluable later on in a future career. I've wanted to get involved in international business/relations and foreign languages for as long as I can remember, but I was never able to see the world from so many different perspectives until I started corresponding internationally. Every letter I receive adds another piece to my jigsaw-puzzle-view of the world.

Many things have changed since I've gotten involved in international correspondence. I have become more knowledgeable about world events. I am an avid stamp collector, and I must be the best customer the post office has ever had. But there is one thing that has remained the same over the years—I'm still the dreamer who wanted to see the world. Only now, some of my dreams are finally starting to come true as I live vicariously through the ink of my foreign friends.

## Comments

The admissions officers generally received this essay well. They commented favorably about the writer's "natural, straightforward style" and the "sweetly conceived, modestly well-executed" essay. One officer noted, "It shows us a person who is eager to learn about different kinds of people, which is exactly the sort of person an admission committee is seeking. She is certainly laying an excellent foundation for her/his future career." Most of the suggestions for improvement centered around the fact that not much actually happens in the essay.

The writer is direct and clear. She takes the reader along for the ride. It's simply not a very exciting one.

She could do one thing to dramatically improve this essay: avoid getting caught up in generalizations. She never really communicates the impact of her statement, "Many things have changed since I've gotten involved in correspondence. . . ." I wanted one real example. I thought this essay was going to be about her friend and some specific instances when the writer learned from her. But, it wasn't. A nice effort, but hardly worth remembering.

It seemed that the student was just getting the essay going and then stopped. The experience was interesting but the evolution of the essay fell short of being a complete work.

## ESSAY 48: Harvard, current affairs/family illness: Medicine
Score: 79

### The Key to Medical Advancement

Throughout the twentieth century, virtually every aspect of modern medicine has reaped the rewards of technological advancements. Society will be forever indebted to those pioneers who conceived the vast array of preventions, treatments, and cures that are readily available to mankind today. Apparently, the imaginations of these pioneers know no boundaries, for every day we are informed of progress in yet another domain of study.

Until recently, relatively little ethical consideration needed to accompany our quest for improvement. Indeed, few can find moral fault with important discoveries such as a polio vaccine and insulin. However, medicine is now venturing into areas, such as genetics, which explore the very core of human existence. Consequently, I believe that if medical advancements in these fields are going to continue to benefit society, we need to consider all possible ethical effects before implementing new discoveries. We must ensure that the potential for abuse will not override the capacity for gain.

One of the biggest breakthroughs in genetics has been the use of bacteria to genetically engineer drugs such as insulin and growth hormone. Five years ago, a brain tumor destroyed my brother's pituitary gland. He now takes genetically engineered growth hormone on a daily basis to replace that which he no longer naturally produces. This technology has helped give back to him a portion of what he lost to the tumor. An effort is currently underway to make growth hormone more readily available to the general public for treatment of ailments such as osteoporosis, severe burns, and infertility. Many people could benefit from growth hormone, but there is also a high probability that it will be abused for athletic purposes. Football great Lyle Alzado appeared on national television appealing to the public to refrain from misusing the growth hormone which he felt was responsible for his brain cancer. Therefore I feel we need to limit how available we make the drug in order to ensure that it does more good than harm.

Research in genetics is also helping us to locate genes which are linked to diseases such as Cystic Fibrosis, Sickle Cell Anemia, and Huntington's disease. The knowledge of these genes may lead to better treatments and maybe even a cure one day. As well, genetics is now being used in amniocentesis tests to determine, for abortion purposes, if an embryo has an abnormality such as the medical condition known as Down's Syndrome.

Giving people the opportunity to abort an unplanned child is an issue all by itself. Giving people the opportunity to abort a planned pregnancy because the child isn't what they wanted is absolutely ludicrous. I am a support worker for a child who has Down's Syndrome. He's every bit as much a human being as you and I, and therefore is entitled to all the privileges that accompany the status. Every day he makes me smile and reminds me of how lucky I am simply to be alive. He is the epitome of the innocence which is all too often absent from our fast-paced lives.

What happens when our knowledge expands, as it inevitably will, and an amniocentesis can test for hair and eye color? Will we abort a pregnancy because the child won't develop blond hair and blue eyes? After all, the argument could be made that a poor physical appearance may cause hardship in life. More importantly, if the technology becomes available, will we custom design children to our specifications by manipulating their genes? Whatever happened to playing the cards we're dealt? If we're not careful we might create another Frankenstein.

Implementing these, and other technologies raises some critical ethical issues. A world war took place over 50 years ago because numerous countries intensely disagreed with Adolf Hitler on some of these same issues. Hitler wanted to create a supreme race and eliminate disabled people such as those having Down's Syndrome. Do we agree with basic principles behind Hitler's intentions and merely disagree with the method he employed? Hitler was one of the most despised men of modern history. Don't look now, but it appears as though we're simply taking a different, more accepted route to the same destination.

Technology seems to be growing at an exponential rate. Every door we open leads to more doors which conceal secrets. The majority of the population can only imagine the excitement of opening one of these doors for the first time ever. The pursuit of this excitement has understandably overwhelmed us. We've been blindly unlocking doors as fast as possible with little concern for what might lie beyond the door. However, if mankind is going to continue to prosper we need to start peering through the keyhole to see what lies beyond the door. Then, and only then, can we catch a glimpse of the pros and cons of opening it.

Until now, the main difficulty in unlocking a door has been finding the right key. Perhaps the true challenge actually lies in deciding which doors should be opened and which doors are better left untouched. The principle consideration in making this decision needs to be the ethics of its potential applications.

## Comments

This applicant took a risky approach by tackling a tough subject—one that would be hard for most college graduates (let alone a high school senior) to write about succinctly. However, the writer made a good effort. As one officer commented, "The author obviously thinks deeply about these important issues, and an admission officer would recognize that this student would probably think deeply about other issues raised in classes." Tackling these big issues brings two inherent risks. First, the subject matter begs a serious approach, and the writer risks coming across as stiff and impersonal. Second, the writer risks getting in over his or her head and can end up making general claims without the experience or ability to back them up.

This student holds incredibly passionate beliefs about the ethics of medical research. But ethics is a slippery topic, far too subjective for the amount of generalizations he has made. The "we need tos" and "we musts" make his assertions a little too final.

The language is a bit stiff and awkward, and the essay tends to ramble.

"Five years ago, a brain tumor destroyed my brother's pituitary gland." This would be a great opening sentence! So why is it buried? Personal experience is always a useful tool for introducing one's own beliefs, much more so than unsupported blanket statements. Had the student begun here, he would have written a stronger essay without having to compromise his position one bit.

In paragraph seven: Be careful! The Holocaust is a loaded example. There was a lot more to it than just eradicating disabilities. Make sure you understand the implications of the parallels you draw.

It is dangerous for a nonprofessional (especially a high school student) to attempt writing as though the essay will be presented at a professional conference. You may be writing to someone who knows much more than you and will be irritated by your hackneyed proclamations. I give my students this advice: "Write small." Keep the topic close to your own life and write only about something you know.

I admire the student for voicing his beliefs, but I'd admire him even more if he had played devil's advocate a bit. One of my former professors always admonished, "Seek the truth in what you oppose and the error in what you espouse." What are the weaknesses in his arguments? Is a technical advancement without extensive debate on the potential ethical pitfalls ever appropriate? Addressing such questions would go a long way in communicating to the admissions committee that the author is an open minded (if steadfast) person.

## ESSAY 49: Harvard, funny/creative: the "Grip Test"
### Score: 75.6

**Describe an accomplishment that was important to you but went unnoticed.**

It's not that I'm a weak guy, just that I had been somewhat self-conscious about my strength early on in my high school career. My gym class didn't help too much, either. Thanks to a demeaning test of strength appropriately dubbed the "Grip Test," once each quarter I was provided the opportunity to squeeze a gadget, get a score, and have my teacher announce it out loud, no matter how high or (as in my case) how low it was. No matter how hard I tried, the cruel and callous scale never registered above 40. Almost every other male in the class could boast of a high-40's or mid-50's score. I hated that test with a passion. Until recently. When this semester rolled around and I had the gripper placed in my palm, I was prepared for the same old same old. I had been improving slightly from quarter to quarter, but nothing impressive ever happened. I drew in a deep breath, squeezed, looked at the scale, and almost fainted. Sixty-six! In a way only a teenager can appreciate, for an accomplishment only a teenager would find meaningful, I thought I was in heaven. My success was even sweeter as I watched jocks pale in comparison when they took the test. Sure, to some people my academic accomplishments seem fairly impressive, and I would agree. Yet the grip test situation was much more personal and represented success in an area I normally don't pay attention to. Plus I learned two things. One: I can pride myself on the smallest triviality. Two: I'm glad we don't measure strength in our gym classes with the bench press.

## Comments

The light style and wit of this essay resonated well with a number of our officers. "Natural, conversational style . . . light touch; humorous, but also makes a good point," commented one. "This is, overall, a nice, direct essay with a straightforward introduction and a self-effacing, mildly humorous conclusion. I get the sense that the writer knows that success and failure both contain elements of caprice," noted another. The reason that it did not receive a higher score is largely due to factors beyond the writer's control. First, the panelists were not aware that this essay was actually part of a set. Second, they were not aware that the school imposed a strict word limit. Had they known that a series of other short pieces focusing on more serious aspects of the writer's life surrounded this essay, they probably would have graded it on a much more lenient scale. (To see the other essays this writer submitted, see essays 16–22.)

Though competent as a writer, his message is a little meek. I'm not exactly sure what I'm supposed to know about him after reading this.

This one may not be the student's fault. The question is lousy; it invites triviality. It's the rare kid who can write with the kind of understatement this topic requires in order for the essay to be a good one. I once worked at a school where we asked students to tell us about a book that had a significant influence on their lives. Over half wrote about a children's book, and only a handful of those essays were worth reading. In other words, it might be nice to point out to readers that colleges sometimes have lame essay questions.

## ESSAY 50: Chicago, international experience/ethnic identity: Italian Meal

Score: 75.4

**Describe your most memorable meal.**

To me, there is nothing better than a good "home-cooked" Italian meal. Keeping this in mind, what could be better than eating such a meal in Italy cooked by relatives that you have never seen before in the medieval village of your ancestors. Two summers ago, I attended just such an event, alone!

I remember it like it was yesterday. It was a hot, muggy Mediterranean day. I was sitting on the steps of Santa Croce Square in Florence waiting for my rented driver to arrive. After becoming one with the pavement, my eyes beheld a dark blue Alfa Romeo pull up in front of me. Upon seeing this, I thought to myself, "This is definitely going to be an experience that I will NEVER forget!" After trying to explain where I wanted to go, we were finally on our way to Monticatini where I was to meet some of my relatives for the first time. To get there, we traveled a steady rate of 85 to 110 mph—and I loved it! After aimlessly looking for the street I hoped was called Via [name], we found the house. Standing there was a man I had never seen before, yet I knew he was related. His name was [name] and he spoke no English. Despite this little difficulty, he was to serve as my tour guide for the rest of the day.

As I walked into the house, I can remember what a strange feeling it was to look on the outside wall and see "[name]" so far away from MY home. I swear that I had to of checked the spelling of the name a thousand times before I was really convinced it was the same. Upon entering the house, I was greeted by some of the others that lived there with a traditional Italian style greeting. Among them was [name], ironically an Italian banker, who was now to take over the driving duties to our final destination—Pontito.

It was now down to the four of us: [name], [name], [name] (a friend to help translate,) and myself who set off by car to the medieval village of my ancestors—Pontito. As we wound up the 8,000 ft of hair-pin curved roads into the mountains, I finally caught sight of the stalwart village. Suddenly, I began to remember when I visited there as a little boy with my parents and brother and how little time I got to spend there. This time, I was determined to enjoy my relatives and the village much more.

After we parked our car and walked into the narrow passageways of the village, [Name] was quick to point out the carved statue of Pontito's founder, my relative. We then proceeded to go to the house where my remaining relatives lived at the present time. At the door, I was greeted by [name], [name], and [name] who, of course, are the relatives who live there. As I walked in, it felt like I was in a time warp. Nothing had changed since I was there as an eight year old boy. It was exactly the same!

After some discussion, we sat down to eat what could very well be the most memorable dinner of my life. At the table, I was joined only by the men of the family. As is accustomed for them, the women, who cooked the meal, were only to serve us as we ate. Before we were served, I asked what in the world the old carved stone ball in the center of the huge wooden table we were eating off of was. To show how old this place is, I was told that it was once used to throw down the mountain at invading villagers who tried to take over Pontito. Do you realize how old that must be?

Finally, as I was looking out of the window into the hazy mountains and valleys below and watched the sun rays bounce off of the stone floor, (electricity was a recent discovery to Pontito, they only had one light bulb,) dinner was served, and served, and served! Not expecting the eight-course meal I was about to receive, I was already full after the first round of pasta. I sat there and watched my relatives put away food like it was water. After a while, somewhere around the prosciutto or the veal courses, they started to ask me why I was not eating everything. I didn't know what to do. I was so full that I was ready to explode but I couldn't explain this to the crying women who thought I hated her food—so I ate! I ate so much food from then on that I couldn't even look at food for the next two days. I even drank two cups of coffee to make her happy, and I HATE coffee! Don't get me wrong, the food was great, but there was enough to feed twenty people.

Another thing that amazed me was how much wine everyone consumed. Between the five men at the table, the drank eight bottles of homemade red wine and weren't even slightly affected! As for me, I was absolutely thrilled to be drinking water that was taken from the natural mountain spring trough once used by my ancestors many, many years ago. It was such pure, untouched water, (although it is said that one of my American relatives when visiting died two minutes after drinking the water for the first time for no apparent reason!)

Then, after eating more food than I can handle in a week, it was time to go. We said our good-byes and proceeded down the mountain to the car. Although desperately trying to keep my eyes awake, I feel asleep until we returned to Monticatini. There, after [name] took me to the local Ferrari dealership, I went to Monticatini Terme where I took a train back to Florence. On that train, I just sat there and tried to grasp the full concept of what had just happened that day. I thought of how fortunate I was to have been able to visit with relatives and trace my heritage back so far. I thought about the graves that I had seen in Pontito with "[name]" etched into them and what those relatives lives must have been like. Now, after I have long since returned to my home in America, I still think about Pontito and that incredible meal I enjoyed there. As I think about it now, the only way that meal can be topped would be to someday see MY children sitting at that same wooden table and experiencing exactly what I did.

## Comments

The applicant needs to work on the writing style. The admissions officers generally liked the story itself. "This is an entertaining story, and I would value the experience that this student would bring to the entering class," said one. However, some on our panel felt that the applicant did not go into enough depth about the actual meal. For instance, one panel member said, "The student writes more about the journey to the meal than the experience of the meal itself. There obviously was more to it than the story tells, and that information would have made the essay far more colorful and interesting."

The author creates an unintended tension in this essay between what he wants us to know and what he actually tells us. Reflecting upon his visit to Pontito as a child, he writes, "This time, I was determined to enjoy my relatives and the village much more." What a fascinating premise for a personal essay! It offers the opportunity for reflection on how he has grown since childhood, on what it means to commune with family in an utterly foreign environment, on the significance of making this visit alone—all framed within the description of a traditional Italian family dinner. And he drops hints throughout the essay that this is what made the visit and the meal significant: the statue of his ancestor who founded Pontito, the sign with his surname on the entrance to the house, the stone ball on the table, the desire to see his children have the same experience. But he never goes any further. Rather than explaining how and why these icons hold real meaning for him, he essentially writes, "This just blows my mind!" In that respect, they have no more significance in this essay than the Alfa Romeo or zipping through the countryside at 100 m.p.h. or the amount of food everyone ate or how much wine they drank or the fact that he managed to choke down two cups of coffee. In other words, because he makes no real distinctions between those things which hold ancestral and cultural relevance to him and those which are trivial by comparison, everything is reduced to the state of being "cool." Not until the final paragraph do we get the sense that he has grown from this experience. I wish he had started there instead; it could have been a powerful essay.

[Beware of] wearisome transitions: "As I walked," "After we parked," "After some discussion," "As I was looking out," "After eating more food."

## ESSAY 51: Harvard, family illness: Mother's Fight with Cancer
### Score: 73

I am learning, both through observations and first-hand experiences, that there are many mishaps in life which seem to be unexplainable and unfair, and yet have devastating consequences. Disease fits into this category. Its atrocity does not stem from the fact that it is a rare or uncommon occurrence, since illness and disease pervade our lives as we hear numerous stories of sick people and come into contact with them each day. However, there is a marked difference between reading in the newspaper that a famous rock star or sports icon has tested H.I.V. positive and discovering that your own mother has been diagnosed with cancer.

Undoubtedly, the most influential people in my life have been my mother and father. It is to them that I credit many of my accomplishments and successes—both inside and outside of school. Throughout my childhood, my parents have always fostered and encouraged me in all my endeavors. At all my sporting events, spelling bees, concerts, and countless other activities, they have always been front row and center. My parents, in conjunction with twelve years of Catholic training, have also instilled in me a sound belief in a loving, caring God, which I have come to firmly believe. It therefore should not come as a surprise that the news of my mothers sickness would greatly alter my entire outlook on life. Where was my God?

My mother, in fact, had been aware of her condition in the spring of my junior year in high school. She deliberately did not inform my sister or me of her illness because she did not want to distract us from our studies. Instead, my mother waited for the completion of her radiation therapy treatments. At this time, she brought me into her room, sat me down on the same wooden rocking chair from which she used to read me bedtime stories, and began to relate her story. I did not weep, I did not flinch. In fact, I hardly even moved, but from that point onward, I vowed that I would do anything and everything to please my mother and make her proud of me.

Every subsequent award won and every honor bestowed upon me has been inspired by the recollection of my mother's plight. I look to her as a driving force of motivation. In her I see the firm, enduring qualities of courage, strength, hope, and especially love. Whenever I feel discouraged or dispirited, I remember the example set by my mother and soon become reinvigorated. Instead of groveling in my sorrow, I think of all the pain and suffering that my mother had to endure and am revived with new energy after realizing the triviality of my own predicament.

For instance, last year, when I was playing in a championship soccer game, my leg became entangled with a forwards leg on the other team, and I wound up tearing my medial cruciate ligament. I was very upset for having injured myself in such a seemingly inane manner. Completely absorbed in my own anguish, I would not talk to anyone and instead lamented on the sidelines. But then I remembered something that my mother used to say to me whenever something like this happened: If this is the worst thing that ever happens to you, I'll be very happy, and you'll be very lucky. Instantly, many thoughts race through my mind. I pictured my mother as a young thirteen-year-old walking to the hospital every day after school to visit her sick father. She had always told me how extremely painful it had been to watch his body become emaciated as the cancer advanced day by day and finally took its toll. I then pictured my mother in the hospital, thirty years later, undergoing all the physically and mentally debilitating tests, and having to worry about her husband and her children at the same time. I suddenly felt incredibly ashamed at how immature I had been acting over my own affliction.

I gathered my thoughts and instead of sulking or complaining, helped coach my team to victory.

I am very happy to say that my mother is now feeling much better and her periodic checkups and C.A.T. scans have indicated that she is doing very well. Nevertheless, her strength and courage will remain a constant source of inspiration to me. I feel confident to greet the future with a resolute sense of hope and optimism.

## Comments

The majority of the suggestions for this essay highlight the danger inherent in relying on an overly poignant topic, in this case the writer's mother's bout with cancer. Part of why the reactions to this piece are so passionate (and why there are so many of them) is because had the applicant just taken a slightly different approach, he could have had a powerful and touching composition on his hands. It is always frustrating when a piece with so much potential misses the mark. In this case, the material and emotion are all there. Had he spent more time and written with more sincerity, this essay might have been a real winner.

I wish this kid had started the essay with his mom sitting him down in the rocking chair. That would have been a powerful beginning. In general, using the introduction of the essay to paint a scene or mood can be very effective.

He should begin with the most simple and striking sentence possible, such as "On January 5, 20XX, my mother learned that she had cancer." Use real times and exact places. Let the most dramatic point go where it belongs, at the end of the sentence—also known as the stress point.

Because this topic is so personal, I yearn to know more about the student's reaction to his mom's cancer, how he and his family dealt with it over time. As written, things just seem a bit too tidy.

The author describes a valuable life lesson, but I find the writing style to be artificial and a bit maudlin. I imagine he resorted to the thesaurus more than once.

The writer tells us a sad story about his mother with cancer and how he has strived to do his best because of what his mother has been through. The topic can be a tear jerker, but this essay lacked the depth and richness that other essays with similar topics possess.

The experience obviously impacted the student very much. But what students do not realize is that they do not have to share such personal issues within the confines of a college essay.

I don't believe the "epiphany" in the conclusion as it's described. It's too easy and convenient to be believable. He begins his description with "For instance," which negates almost everything that follows. When he sees his mother in his mind, he "instantly" thinks this and "suddenly" does that, and finally "helped coach his team to victory." He "coached" the team. "Cheered" maybe. "Coached?" No way.

This essay smells of contrivance. Yes, his mother's bout with cancer affected him. Just not in the way he wants me to believe. This is the "lasting sanctifying effect" essay. Look at what the writer is actually saying (using his own words): I used to be "absorbed in my own anguish" and "lament" my bouts with adversity. But, "instantly" or "suddenly" (take your pick), I became a young man "confident to greet the future with a resolute sense of hope and optimism." Why not say, "I used to be a thoughtless, immature teenager. My mother got cancer. I'm now a thoughtful, mature adult. You should admit me to _____." His essay is no less subtle.

## ESSAY 52: Penn, achievement: Running for Student Government
Score: 73

**Please cite and discuss a quotation, phrase, or statement that has had an influence on your life.**

My brother once told me "If you don't choose someone for a job and they don't show up the next day, you made the right decision: they didn't care enough about the job to stick around." Repeatedly, I have found it necessary to prove myself to people who have denied me what I sought. I realized the truth of my brother's statement after losing two class elections to the same opponent, at the beginning and end of my freshman year in high school.

My first loss was devastating. I wanted to win the office to make myself known in my new school. I was ambitious to be special; not just one of the 2,200 students roaming the halls. However, I lost the election, and all I could do about it was swallow my pride and shake my opponent's hand. Congratulations!

I remembered my brother's statement, and decided not to let my fellow students be correct in judging me unworthy of the job I wanted, so I devoted most of my spare time to the Student Government, and at the end of the year, I decided to run again. This time I would not fail. But once again, my ambitions were crushed as my brother, the current president of the Student Government, looked at me sorrowfully and sighed as he announced the name of the winner. All I could do was swallow my tears and shake my opponent's hand. Congratulations, again!

Once more, I decided it was worthwhile to make my contributions to the school without the title of office, and when election time rolled around the following year, I let it pass. It was during these two years that I accomplished the thing of which I am most proud: the creation of a new Student Constitution. I had realized that I didn't need a title to make a difference. Yet, I felt that I must make one final attempt to win an office; I wanted recognition for the work I had done, and the opportunity to be in a position where I could do more. Finally, I succeeded.

My opponent did not shake my hand. Nor did she show up the next day. I guess my colleagues had finally made the right decision.

## Comments

This essay received a wide range of comments. It might have made it into our mixed bag category had a consensus not said that the tone of the essay needed improvement. This is a case where an attempt to write with passion, conviction, and confidence crosses the line and ends up looking like superiority and cockiness instead. This applicant probably would have benefited from getting more feedback. Still, some of our panelists saw through to the applicant's good qualities and did admire his determination and persistence.

I like this essay, even with its errors, because it tells a personal story of determination. Every detail, from the brother's quote in the introduction to the specific examples of effort and achievement, is personal. The combination of the details creates a picture of a tenacious student who learned from defeat, fortified his efforts, and continued toward the original goal. The fact that the student eventually won the election is not really important, although it's nice to know the effort paid off.

I understand that the author is trying to establish that he is willing to do the work required behind the scenes to make things happen at school. However, the attitude that comes across is still one of self-righteous indignation. The author never did really get over feeling miffed that he lost the elections. . . . And the impression of moral superiority over the vanquished opponent who didn't show up to work the next day is unattractive. Although the essay is well written technically, it conveys an immaturity that would make an admission officer wonder if this person would actually be pleasant to work with.

The student neglected to fully develop his topic. There was a lack of real effort put into the creative writing part of the process.

I had to reread the quote on which this essay is based four or five times for it to make sense. And I am still only guessing.

The story of creating a new Student Constitution might be worth reading. But the writer assumes that because "creation of a new constitution" is so high sounding, the reader will be automatically impressed. Nothing has meaning in and of itself. If the writer doesn't tell the story, nothing of substance remains.

## ESSAY 53: Columbia, childhood experience: A Brothers' Argument
Score: 73

Of the many ironies which exist in life, one stands out in my mind: the same information which you would like to attain from others if often the same knowledge they would least like to divulge. As competition continues to grow in all areas, many who strive for an advantage must act tactfully and follow Polonius's advice in Hamlet that states, "By indirections find directions out" (II, i, L. 65). A perfect example comes to mind.

In the midst of another swaggeringly hot [home state] summer, I remember my brother's voice getting louder and louder and harsher and harsher as he repeatedly asked me, "Where is it? Where is it?" With his patience finally at an end, [brother's name] came running after me. Before I could get out of the room, my brother was on top of me, and i was screaming out in pain that I couldn't breathe. Luckily he felt a reasonable amount of mercy that day and let me go. But I still didn't tell him.

I had hidden his present for a very legitimate reason, at least, to a stubborn seven-reason year old.

I hailed "Monkey," the cutest thing ever sewn, as one of my three sacred pocessions along with my gameboy and my tennis racquet. No one had ever seen one like him—that is until [brother's name]'s tenth birthday, when he unwrapped a beige stuffed monkey of the exact same make. Apparently my brother had asked for one, and with good intentions in mind, my parents complied. But little [brother's name] would not have it. The moment I was left alone in [brother's name]'s room, I took the newest addition to his stuffed animal collection and hid it inside the old, seldom-used rice cooker with the intent of suffocating it, and hoped someone would cook it.

Tired of the enormous racket, my father decided to solve the problem. At first he tried to reason with me as if I were mature enough to understand that I had no right to hide my brother's things and not give them back. Getting absolutely nowhere, my dad tried a more sophisticated approach.

"You're afraid I'll laugh at your bad hiding spot," my father claimed.

"[brother's name] couldn't find it, " I replied convincingly.

"How smart can a seven year-old be? I could probably find hundreds of better places—under a couch, in a drawer."

I began to feel angry that my own father thought I was that dumb. "Certainly not in a better place than behind the T.V., " he continued.

"Uh-huh. I put it in the old rice cooker!" I proclaimed emphatically.

"Wow, [my name]! You're a real genius, " my father exclaimed in astonishment.

I felt so good after surprising my dad that I completely forgot about my anger over my brother's gift. It wasn't until I couldn't find my own monkey that night that I realized I had been tricked.

I learned an extremely valuable lesson from this commonplace childhood event. It often proves advantageous to find out others' secrets at the same time that I am protecting my own. For example, one of my numerous goals during a tennis match warm-up is to discover my opponent's game plan while I conceal mine. I do not, however, see deviousness as something to be used detrimentally toward others, rather, as a tool to be used for personal and team gain. If I want something in life, I have to lead others, and get it myself. One big step toward achievement is staying alert not to be on the receiving end of manipulation. Sadly, I have since lost "Monkey," but his memories and the important lesson he helped teach will always remain with me.

## Comments

Almost every officer who had a suggestion for this essay mentioned the introduction as the primary problem area. Each found the childhood story to be sweet and entertaining. However, as one officer noted, "This is a simple story that needs a simple style of writing. The author is trying too hard to impress."

This essay begins with an awkwardly written pseudoprofundity. "What the heck is he talking about?" is my immediate reaction.

I can do without the gratuitous quote from Hamlet. Please! The question was not, "How many intellectual push-ups can you do?" It would have been much better to begin with his brother's pleading. Like this: "'Where is it?' my brother yelled. But, I wouldn't answer. 'Where is it?' he screamed. I made a dash for the door, but he cut me off, threw me to the floor and landed on top of me." Placing a question at the beginning of an essay is a great hook for catching the reader's attention.

Machiavelli aside, the student takes too long to get to the story, and the story takes too long to get to the point.

## ESSAY 54: Chicago, hobbies and interests: Math, Computers, Sports, and Volunteering
Score: 73

Everyone has met people who can say a few important-sounding, pretentious sentences on a wide variety of subjects, but in reality know little about any of them. Those people are usually termed superficial—whereas they may have heard of a lot of things, they are experts in none. Superficial, in my opinion, is the worst label a person can deserve. Therefore, in everything I do, I strive to achieve as much depth and perfection as possible. While I may not be involved in a great number of wide-ranging activities, I try to perform to the utmost of my abilities in the ones I do participate.

I have had a lifelong fascination with mathematics, a fascination that I perhaps owe to my mother, who has a degree in mathematics and who encouraged me to study it extensively. Mathematics attracts me because of its absoluteness and perfection—it is entirely created by men and therefore can be shaped by the mathematician as he wishes within mathematical rules; on the other hand, the rules of logic are the final judge—there can be no differing opinions in mathematics. In Russia, since second grade I attended an evening math club. I also participated in a number of mathematics competitions and performed fairly well, and was admitted into a prestigious school with a specialization in mathematics. When my family moved to the United States, it became harder for me to pursue my mathematical interests because of the culture and language and my family's financial situation. Nevertheless, I led my school two years in the AHSME competition, making it to the AIME round in 10th grade. Last year I learned about the U.S.A. mathematical talent search competition and participated in it, earning a certificate of completion, being a commended solver on a number of occasions, and attending their summer Young Scholars Program last summer. Finally, this year I organized a team for Mandelbrot Competition, a mathematics competition with both in individual and team components, in my school.

Since coming to the United States, I have also been very interested in computers. In fact, we bought a computer before we bought our second car. I learned several programming languages on my own, including Pascal, C, and C++. In the summer following the 9th grade, I attended Johns Hopkins' Center for Talented Youth program, enrolling in a course entitled Data Structures and Algorithms. And last year, as a member of the Engineering Club, I used my knowledge of computers and programming to help design and program a Programmable Logic Controller, which was part of our design.

After academics, sports are the most important part of my life. I enjoy playing any sport, whether indoor or outdoor, for a team or just for fun, but soccer remains my greatest love. To a kid from Russia, soccer is what baseball or basketball is to an American kid. I have played soccer since I was a kid, and while most of the time it was simply for recreation, my competitive spirit made anything less than winning unacceptable. I have been a starter on the varsity soccer team since my sophomore year, and this year I finally realized my goal—a winning season, and a berth, if not a victory, in the conference finals—with the knowledge that I contributed to this success, being the second-leading scorer on the team. On the other hand, I've only started playing tennis three years ago, after I came to the U.S. While I had always liked the sport, the un-availability of courts in Russia made it impossible for me to practice it while I was there. However, I've been fairly successful since starting to play. I earned a spot on the varsity tennis team in my sophomore year and was named Most Improved Player that year, becoming the regular fifth seed by the end of the season. Last season, in my junior year, I was the regular third, and at times second, seed, and advanced to the semi-finals of the Individual Conference Championships.

I have also tried to help my community. Last year I did volunteer work at HIAS, a Jewish immigrant agency that helps new Jewish families to adjust to the American culture and lifestyle. In addition to office duties, I used my knowledge of Russian to help work with those families who did not speak English. I have further used my knowledge of computers to set up the agency's database system, as well as restoring their comput-ers after a crash.

In whatever I have tried to do, I have tried to excel and to perform to the best of my abilities, and I hope to do the same at the University of Chicago.

## Comments

This essay is very well structured with a well-defined introduction and conclu-sion, focused paragraphs, and good transitions. This essayist did not receive a higher score simply because he tried to do too much in too short a space. Had he chosen just one of these areas (math, computers, sports, or volunteer activi-ties) and written about it in depth, he would have combined his good sense of structure with a clearly defined focus and ended up with a stellar piece.

This should simply begin, "I have a lifelong fascination with mathematics." Skip the introduction and just tell the story!

If I were actually evaluating it in light of this student's entire application, I would cut him some slack. I would take into account the fact that he is from Rus-sia. If you take that into consideration, his command of the English language is actually quite good. Also, presume that he is applying for a math program, and his essay establishes that he is quite good in math, and equally important, he loves it! Finally, he lets us know that he spends time contributing to his community.

Tells me little more than I would otherwise get from a list of extracurricular activities.

This was an "I did this and I did that" type of essay. This essay seemed to be derived from the student's list of extracurricular activities. Essays should be about more than a running tally of accomplishments. It is obvious that this student is quite intelligent and involved, so I find this attempt at a college essay rather baffling. I definitely would expect more from a student who obviously has the academic ability to succeed.

## ESSAY 55: Harvard, family/ethnic identity: Saudi Arabian
### Score: 72

Like many Saudi Arabians, I consider my family an extremely significant part of my life. Being the sixth child out of seven, I have been fortunate enough to be surrounded by a loyal, encouraging family throughout my life. Consequently, I believe nothing has affected me more than the support of my family.

The strong loyalty within my family has allowed me to overcome several obstacles. Of these hardships, two stand out in particular. First, as a member of a traditional Saudi Arabian family in the United States, I was forced to juggle American and Saudi culture throughout most of my life. However, because of the strong support from my family, I have managed to balance the two contrasting cultures. As a result, this support has allowed me to maintain my Saudi heritage while interacting within American culture. The second, and most important, obstacle I have overcome with the help of my family is my lack of a father. My father, currently living in Saudi Arabia, moved there when I was three years old. To compensate for his absence, my four oldest siblings (currently 33, 31, 30, and 27) filled the vacant paternal role in my upbringing. Through this act, my siblings, whom I now regard as surrogate parents, not only raised me successfully, but also instilled in me a sense of strong familial loyalty.

In addition to helping me overcome several major obstacles, the strong loyalty within my family has also affected many parts of my character. One effect of these familial bonds is the sense of selflessness which they have ingrained in me. By constantly witnessing my siblings putting the needs of the family ahead of their own, I learned to do the same. This sense of selflessness has motivated me to help others outside of the family as well. Along with selflessness, the loyalty within my family has given me self-confidence. This self-confidence, stemming from years of trust and support, has allowed me to experiment with many different ideas throughout my life, gaining knowledge along the way. Moreover, this self-confidence is responsible for my optimistic outlook and general feeling of joy.

In conclusion, I believe nothing has benefited me more than the support and loyalty within my family. Consequently, my feelings of loyalty have spread to include not only my family, but also my friends, my school, and my community. At Harvard, I sincerely hope to provide others with the same type of bond which has meant so much to me.

## Comments

The reason that the admissions officers gave for giving this essay the lowest ranking is that it is impersonal and "doesn't reveal much about the writer." Though the writer asserts that he has a number of qualities that he learned from his family (self-confidence and the ability to straddle two cultures, for example) he never backs up these claims with any evidence. He would have vastly improved his piece had he chosen only one quality to focus on and then demonstrated how his family fostered it. How exactly does he straddle two cultures? Illustrating the differences between the two could have made for a fascinating piece.

Note, however, that this essayist does do a number of things well. He has a keen sense of structure and organization, for example, and gives the impression of being a very serious, family-oriented individual.

This essay doesn't tell me much about what this student will bring to the campus community. I presume that he wants us to understand that the values he acquired through his family will generalize to his life at college. All that it tells me, however, is that he considers himself a nice person.

I have always been a bit leery of essays that stress so much the loyalty to one's family. College is a time for loosening ties to family somewhat, and learning to think and act independently. Please understand that I am not, by any means, criticizing love and loyalty to one's family. But an admission officer will want to feel sure that the applicant will be able to establish a vibrant life in an environment far removed from the immediate family.

This essay is one idea restated over and over again. I understand that it was written by an E.S.L. applicant. But that's no excuse for this repetitious writing.

The topic of the essay could have been expanded and explored far more deeply.

It's too bad, if the student had taken more time to create a solid piece, it could have been quite interesting to read. Instead it falls short of the mark.

## Grab Bag

The following essays are not graded and ranked, but all were accepted at the Ivy League schools indicated. They are provided here as additional examples of the quality of writing seen by the admissions committees that will also judge your writing. Our authors have offered brief opinions on how each could have been improved. We hope that these examples will inspire you to produce your best writing, and eventually lead to your acceptance at the school of your choice.

## ESSAY 56: Stanford

We were 12 and we were lost. We were surrounded by adults and we couldn't understand a word that they were saying. We were finally realizing our situation, lost thousands of miles from home in a foreign land where few of the residents spoke English; we panicked. We suddenly found ourselves frantically running around Mozart's birthplace trying to figure out where our tour group had gone. I was terrified. I believed I would never see my family again. Moments before, when eating at a local restaurant, delighting in wienerschnitsel and apple strudel, certain things seemed set in place. In a week, I would return to the U.S., my parents would be waiting for me, ready to bring me home to my own comfortable room. I would show them the neat souvenirs I had bought and the cool pictures I took on the second trip (the picture enclosed is one such picture). I'd get to play with my friends, read my comics and watch television. I would always be protected and I had nothing to fear.

It was just a simple wrong turn, yet I would be ever changed by the experience. We did eventually find our tour group, but I could not return to my own innocent way of thinking before I got lost. My illusions of security and safety had been shattered. This experience deeply reinforced for me the unpredictability of existence; certain events occur and one can't do anything about them. I was awakened to the presence of an ignorant nonchalance with which many kids approach life. I learned to be more aware of how well I have had it, and I became more nervous. I always believed that I would grow up to have a successful happy life, when in actuality, one minor accident or freak event could change my entire world.

This change in attitude and belief has pervaded my personal life and has allowed me to endure stressful incidents and see the linear progression of our lives and the world as a whole. For instance, this past year, while playing in the second game of the varsity football season, I received a blow to the chin which necessitated a visit to the hospital and 18 stitches; I also had to sit out for three weeks while my wound healed. During this time, our team faced one of the toughest opponents we would ever play against. I had to sit idly by as I watched my team lose a close game by a single touchdown. Many times since, I have reflected upon whether or not our team would have won if I had been there in the game to help out. Perhaps if I would have been healthy, I could have made the saving tackle, or I could have made the key block for a tying touchdown. Yet, the knowledge gained in Germany has helped me recognize that there was nothing I could do. I couldn't second guess my actions or those of the team. I had learned in Austria that the actions of the past cannot be reversed and sometimes, life does not proceed as planned. The future is not set in stone, and we are not destined for greatness; we must make the best of the current time and be ready for anything life must throw at us.

## Comments

The author should have provided more detail about what happened between the wrong turn and being reunited with her tour group. Generally, it is best to focus on how an event has influenced you, as opposed to the event itself. However, this applicant has made sweeping statements about her new outlook and the way she approaches situations based on an event that she never explains with any detail. We've all been lost a time or two, and most of us don't experience life-altering perspectives from it. She should have explained why the experience affected her so monumentally (or so she claims). The essay lacks detail, and the author's statements regarding change aren't backed up by good examples.

## ESSAY 57: Harvard

"Unutterable and nameless is that which torments and delights my soul and is also the hunger of my belly."

So says Nietzsche when asked to describe his virtue, but I shall perhaps have to be more specific. My interests have blossomed and deepened over the past few years, until it is difficult for me to spend the amount of time I would like with any of them.

I have always enjoyed advanced mathematics, and I was one of the thirty-two Georgia students who served on last year's ARML state math team, which competed against teams from across the country. The most long-standing of my projects concerns investigations into chaos theory, a relatively new branch of mathematics made possible by the computational power of modern computers. Chaos has recently become popular for the amazingly beautiful fractal images it produces. Several years ago I discovered a new strange attractor (a type of dynamical system based on nonlinear equations); only a dozen or so were known at that time. I have continued my research into developing a general classification system for strange attractors, creating in the process a computer program which can generate several thousand new attractors per hour. This research recently won first place at the State Science Fair.

The summer after my sophomore year I attended the six-week Governor's Honors Program in mathematics. We were also allowed to pick a minor area to study, and I chose literature. Since then I have developed an immense interest in literature and writing. I helped last year to produce the student literary journal, and this year I am serving as chief editor. My interest in writing springs from the joy inherent in creating a construction where beauty and complexity intertwine, and it will likely be lifelong.

Last summer a close friend and I worked to develop a new constitution for student government. The existing student council was ineffectual and unrepresentative; we designed a political structure to revitalize the procedures and spirit of student government in meeting the student body's needs. I now serve as the Parliamentarian for that body, as well as being active in Key Club, National Honor Society, and the Beta Club, of which I am president.

My chief interest lately has been philosophy, in particular the metaphysical explorations of the fundamental nature of existence. The study is time-consuming and often tedious, but is well worth it when one finally grasps what Heidegger means in his discussion on the relationship between man and the ultimate ground of Being. For the past year, I have been active as the youngest participant in the Humanities Forum, a program which offers weekly classes taught by philosophy professors from Emory and other area colleges. The ultimate questions haunt my thoughts, and I must do all I can to surmount them. The task may require a lifetime; I will have lost the day to gain eternity.

I have maintained straight A's throughout my scholastic career; last year I was awarded the Harvard Book Award, and I will soon graduate as the Valedictorian of [name] High School. I was recently named STAR Student for [name] City Schools, and I am a National Merit Scholar for 1995. Next year, at college I am not yet sure of my concentration, but I am leaning towards English or philosophy; whatever the choice, I hope to be able to satisfy the wide scope of my interests.

## Comments

This essay could have begun with paragraph 3. The first two paragraphs are forced introductions that do not add to the overall effectiveness of the essay. The transition sentences are ineffective and the essay lacks cohesiveness. It is impersonal and likely to bore an admissions committee. It includes many topics that can be found elsewhere on the submitted application. The admissions committee will not get to know the applicant through this essay. Although it did not keep the applicant out of Harvard, the essay did not enhance the application.

## ESSAY 58: Brown

I consider myself privileged: born in New York City, raised there and in Boston and Geneva, Switzerland, I have lived in cosmopolitan cities all my life. Yet, this is not the limit of my exposure to diversity, as my parents come from cultures as different as hot and cold, one English and one Indian. So I was planted, a hybrid seed, in the fertile soil of my home life, and the urban environment nurtured the multiculturalism in me, to make me what I am.

The international school that I went to during my four years in Geneva literally opened up a whole world of experiences to me. There were 96 nationalities represented in the school, and my friends belonged to most of them. I noticed an interesting fact about the school: every student, while he related to people from his own country, did not mix exclusively with them. Here, one was not judged by where one came from, but by the quality of one's character. Even when countries were at war with one another, the children of those countries would no think twice about hanging out with their "enemies." Since many of the students were children of diplomats or high-ranking government personnel, this indifference to nationalities was refreshing and reassuring in light of future global interdependence. Furthermore, the issue of color was not an issue at all in the school. Of the little amount of discrimination that there was, the color of one's skin was the very least of this. Yet, unfortunately, this particular lack of prejudice does not exist in America, and is, in fact, one of the greatest hurdles we, as a society, must leap.

In retrospect, the International School showed me a society that has not prepared me for life in the Untied States, for it has shown me a society that not only tolerated, but thrived on ethnic, religious, and racial differences. On the other hand, I feel equipped, not only from my experiences, but also out of my personal beliefs, for the America of tomorrow, where diversity will be commonplace.

Throughout my life, I have learned a few of the skills which will help cope with a vastly changing population. For example, I have learned another language, and hope to learn more in college. I have learned never to judge anyone on any ethnic basis. I have learned the value and interest of not only my own varied background, but of those around me too. I am aware, too, that it is necessary to be able to deal with racism when confronted with it, in such a way as to defuse the situation rather than incite it. America has been called a melting pot, but I prefer to think of it as a stir fry, where all people are mixed together, but retain their original flavors.

## Comments

The strength of this essay is the insight it offers into the applicant's high school years abroad. Although it could have been more personal, it does at least describe a unique experience from the applicant's past that had huge influences on who he is today. The essay had a couple of typos that should have been resolved before it was submitted. The main downside is the weakness that the applicant draws attention to when saying that his multicultural high school had "not prepared me for life in the United States." To indicate that the color blindness he grew up surrounded by may leave him vulnerable in a culture where prejudices still abound may leave the admissions committee to wonder if he will be able to handle life at their school. The essay would have been stronger if he had focused on the strengths of his multicultural upbringing and not just on its uniqueness.

## ESSAY 59: Cornell

I have a simple accomplishment. Whether it is outstanding or not is for the beholder to decide. Two of my poems are going to be published. The endeavor itself was not incredibly grueling; I merely had to type up two of my poems and send them to a publisher. Quite uncomplicated. However, the precursor to that stamped envelope was altogether extraordinary.

Creating those poems was indeed a remarkable task. My poetry is very enigmatic (or so people say), and yet every poem seems simple, almost shallow. However, every one has a deeper meaning, a meaning closer to my mind or my heart or my emotion. Poetry does not always flow freely inside my skull as some believe; every poem and every stanza and every word is drawn from a single, brief, shimmering moment of inspiration in which terrible emotion streams forth through my pencil on to the immaculate whiteness of the page. Every poem of mine that is shared is a fragment of my essence released from my being. As I printed those final words, those closing passions, a wonderful exhaustion diffused through my form. I had found the end of a powerful deluge.

Often I contemplate the significance of such a liberation of fervor, of turmoil. As others feel the published pages and see the words they contain, that audience will assimilate discreet bits of my persona, modest traces of my character. I will brush every individual that reads those poems. And in that, I will be immortal.

## Comments

The essay's strengths are that it is brief and focused. It most likely received mixed reviews from the admissions committee. The language seems a bit contrived—atypical of casual conversation, which is the tone that most admissions officers admit wanting to read. Whether or not it is representative of the author's true feelings, the tone gives off a pretentious vibe.

# Essay Index

Are you looking for inspiration in a particular area? Do you want to find essays written by students with similar interests to your own? Would you like to compare essays written by students accepted to the same or different schools? Use this index to help you locate specific essays throughout the book that pertain to particular subject areas and schools.

## Sorted by Subject

## Sorted by School

# Interviewing the Interviewers

**This is a book about writing essays—why include information about interviewing?**

This is a good question with a simple answer. The interview and the essay have a lot in common. Much of the research that you did to write your essays will be enormously helpful to you when you find yourself fielding questions face-to-face with an admissions officer. Likewise, a lot of the same advice applies. Be yourself, give the interviewer details, be honest, and tell a story or two. Stories are as important to a good interview as they are to a good essay.

Also, like the essays, the interview is something that you can still control. It is never too late to prepare for and learn about giving terrific interviews. Also like the essay, the interview gives your application a face and a personality. It makes you more memorable.

Plus, we gathered a panel of admissions officers from top schools who were ready and willing to share all their wisdom and advice with us. To not have asked them for some tips about the interview process while we had them in front of us would have been remiss.

Below you will find the results of our interview with the interviewers. Keep their advice in mind as you prepare. You may even find yourself looking forward to the opportunity to get to know and connect with the people on the other side of the admissions door.

## 1) How important is the interview?

*The interview is another opportunity to be different from other students with the same credentials. They are the opportunity for the students to use their own words to express themselves in person. It is a terrific, huge opportunity. The mere effort of it impresses colleges.*

*Seize every opportunity for an interview, from high school visits and local alumni interviews to campus interviews and college fairs. Believe it or not, we do keep track of all of this. If there are two kids in the same high school with the same credentials, the student who made the effort will be admitted.*

*Colleges don't require interviews because they can't interview every applicant. But someone who definitely has blips to explain should be interviewed. You need to take the opportunity to explain away the inconsistencies.*

**"Will an Interview Help?"**

*I can't tell you how many times I've been asked this question.*

*"Of course," I reply. "But it can hurt, too." Look at the form of the question. It's designed to affirm a belief, not elicit an honest answer. Students, but more often parents, should disabuse themselves of the notion that merely meeting someone improves their chances of admission.*

*One good example of this is a young woman whose parents flew her all the way from the West Coast for an interview. My first question was, "What classes are you taking this semester?" She couldn't remember. This disaster was a by-product of the almost superstitious belief applicants have in their own power to make an impression in an interview. This young woman was committed to meeting me, not to discuss her own life. She was stumped by the first and simplest question. Though not as extreme, it happens all the time.*

## 2) What qualities do you look for in an interviewee?

*Students who can be themselves and let their personalities and interests shine through.*

*Students who can take a question and turn the interview into a discussion or conversation with depth and clarity of thought.*

*Students who are truly engaging.*

*Those who can articulate their interest in your institution and can tell you why they would fit in.*

*Individual expression is the key to a great interview. When students are confident in themselves and their ideas/ideals, it makes for an engaging conversation instead of having a number of questions asked then answered without any flow of discussion.*

## 3) What are some common interview pitfalls?

*Don't reiterate the college catalog/viewbook to the interviewer. Find the areas within the viewbook or catalog that you have the most interest in and speak to that topic.*

*Being unprepared to discuss themselves, their past, their likes and dislikes, dreams and goals for the future in detail.*

*Being overprepared can be your downfall in an interview. There are students who try to prepare for questions that they think they are going to be asked, and when they are not asked the questions that they prepared for, then they are stumped.*

## 4) Does it *really* matter what applicants wear?

*Go into the interview as yourself and not what you think the interviewer is expecting. Do not wear that suit or dress if you are not comfortable. Be confident and dress how you want to be remembered, hopefully as an individual.*

*First impressions are important but are not always accurate when it comes to 17- and 18-year-old students. You could have a student dressed in Brooks Brothers who could not tell you what he/she had for breakfast. You could also have a student dressed in Birkenstocks and wrinkled clothes but who could explain the atmospheric pressure on Saturn.*

*How they look doesn't matter, it's how they carry themselves. Don't slouch, don't stare out the window, don't pick at your scabs, don't tie your shoes, DO NOT PICK UP anything on the interviewer's desk. Focus.*

## 5) What is your biggest pet peeve when interviewing?

*When a student comes into an interview and tells you what they think you want to hear.*

*Interviewees who do not know the mechanics of a proper greeting with an adult. Too many simply don't know the basics of introducing themselves and don't understand the importance of remembering the interviewer's name.*

*When a student is more interested in their watch or looking out the window than in the conversation.*

*When a student tries to tell you their life story in 15 minutes or less without much direction.*

*An aimless talker.*

## 6) What question(s) do you always ask during an interview?

*If I were to ask your friends to describe you, what adjectives would they use and why?*

*Given your academic and/or extracurricular interests, what is the area(s) that you have the most passion for?*

*What thing(s) excite you about this college/university?*

*Why do you want to attend this school?*

*Is there one question you were hoping I would ask you during the interview? If so, ask it of yourself and answer it for me.*

*"Why?" (As a follow-up to almost every other question.)*

### Answering "Why?"

*Someone once asked me what the hardest question I had ever asked in an interview was and I said "Why?"*

*She replied, "Because I want to know."*

*"No," I said. "The most difficult question I ask is 'Why.'"*

*I've been amazed at how many students see "Why?" as a trick question. I think people expect, "If Plato were a fencer would he use the foil, the épée, or the saber?" Nope. It's just little old "Why?" Of everything you do and enjoy for a while, ask "Why?" and answer it. A detailed thoughtful answer to that question can do more to set you apart than anything else. There is no right answer, but there are well-constructed answers. Be ready for it. "Really?" is another good question that serves as a corollary to "Why?" and makes you avoid unnecessary exaggeration. "It was the worst day of my life!" "Really?"*

*I intentionally look for an interviewee's ability to answer the question "Why?" If I ask, "What's your favorite book?" you better believe "Why?" is going to follow. Interviewees who can go beyond gross generalizations will make a striking impression.*

## 7) What advice would you give to applicants?

*Keep in mind that you want to do an intentional interview. Have some information ready to offer the interviewer, and be ready to answer questions. Many students are so nervous that they give very short answers, yes and no, as if they didn't know they would be asked questions.*

*Above all, be prepared to talk about what you think you are looking for. You don't have to know for sure. Why are you taking the time to interview at this school? A lot of what makes an applicant successful is whether they know what the college is about and how they are a good fit with that college.*

*Colleges that offer evaluative interviews are offering students a chance to fill in the blanks that come up in an application, to become a three-dimensional person, and to talk to someone who is part of the admissions process. One gauge is whether students can articulate what they need from a college. Just show that you have thought or are thinking about these things, not that you've decided.*

*Specific information is always better than general. I'm reminded of a line from Shakespeare's* Othello *when the main character, who is obsessed with proving things objectively, demands of his wife that she prove what she is saying, "Show me thy thought!" That is a good rule to follow: "Show me thy thought." As Othello demands later in the play, "Make me to see it."*

*When students go into an interview, there must be three things they feel the interviewer must know about them before it's all over. There is no excuse for emerging from the interview with the aching feeling that you were cheated by not being given the chance to say the truly important things you had hoped.*

## Five Steps to Interview Preparation

### 1. Look at your entire application objectively

If you were the interviewer, what impressions would you have about the person? Do you see any areas of potential weakness or any red flags that need explaining? Make a list of the kinds of questions that you would ask someone with your background, then practice answering them out loud.

## 2. Reread your essay

A lot of interviewers focus on the essay or use it as the ice breaker. Look at it objectively, and try to imagine what more you would want to know about the writer. Be ready to discuss in depth anything you have written about or even mentioned in the personal statement. If your interview and essay do not back up each other, you will come across as insincere, or worse, dishonest.

## 3. Decide on at least three key points that you want to communicate to the interviewer

Practice making these points by speaking into a tape recorder. Think of ways to incorporate your points into answers for different questions. Use these points to tackle the open-ended questions. Do not leave the interview without feeling confident that you have communicated all three.

## 4. Be prepared with a list of questions you want to ask the interviewers

You do not need to ask more than a few, but have enough questions prepared so that you have some to fall back on if the interviewer addresses some of them before you have had a chance to ask. Take the time to think of the questions that shed further light on what is important to you. Do not ask anything that you could easily look up or find in the view book. You should not need to ask questions just because you have to or because you know the interviewer expects it.

## 5. Be prepared to answer, as well as ask, questions about the school

Refer back to the research you did earlier for your essays. What features drew you to the school? Select key points and criteria, and then prepare your questions. Demonstrate your knowledge of the school and the level of your commitment to it with the depth of your knowledge.

# Index

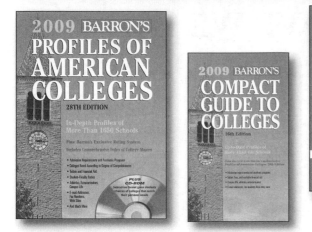